D1068502

Kingfisher

# Learning Adventure Library

SOUTHWESTERN

This edition published in 1996 by
**The Southwestern Company UK ltd**
Goldsmiths House,
Broad Plain, Bristol BS2 OJP
by arrangement with Larousse plc
First published by Larousse plc 1994

Reprinted 1998



A CIP catalogue for this book is available from the British Library

ISBN 0 87197 444 4

Printed in France

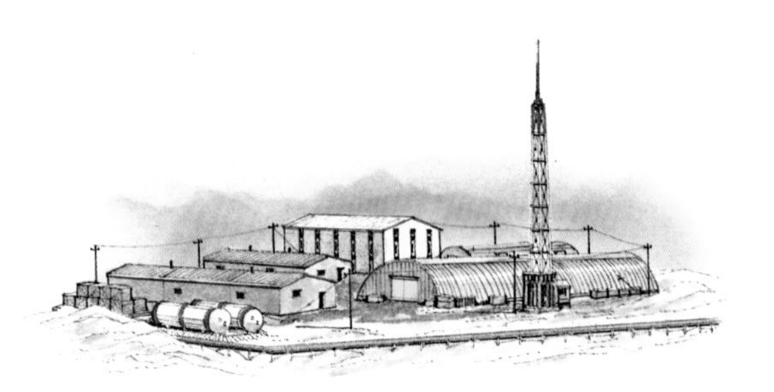

Editor: Catherine Headlam
Designers: Terry Woodley and John Jamieson
Consultant: Keith Lye
Cartographic reference by Andrew Thompson
Additional research by Andrea Moran and Michael Butterworth
Map illustrations by Eugene Fleury (all political maps and the climate map); John Woodcock (all picture maps)
Additional illustrations by Maggie Brand (Maggie Mundy Illustrators Agency); Stephen Conlin; Jeremy Gower (B L Kearley Ltd); Janos Marffy (Kathy Jakeman Illustration): Adam Marshall; Josephine Martin (Garden Studio); Ralph Orme; Clare Roberts (Garden Studio); Roger Stuart; Joanna Williams (B L Kearley Ltd)

# Contents

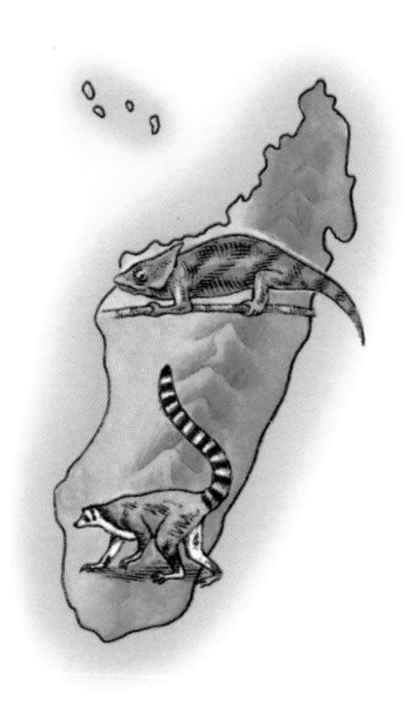

# About this Atlas

Most of the world's land is divided up into seven large continents. In this atlas, six of the continents are shown twice. The first map shows all of the independent countries within each continent. (An independent country is one with its own government.) And the second map shows the major rivers, lakes and mountains. The seventh continent, Antarctica, has just one map. This is because there are no people living there all year round.

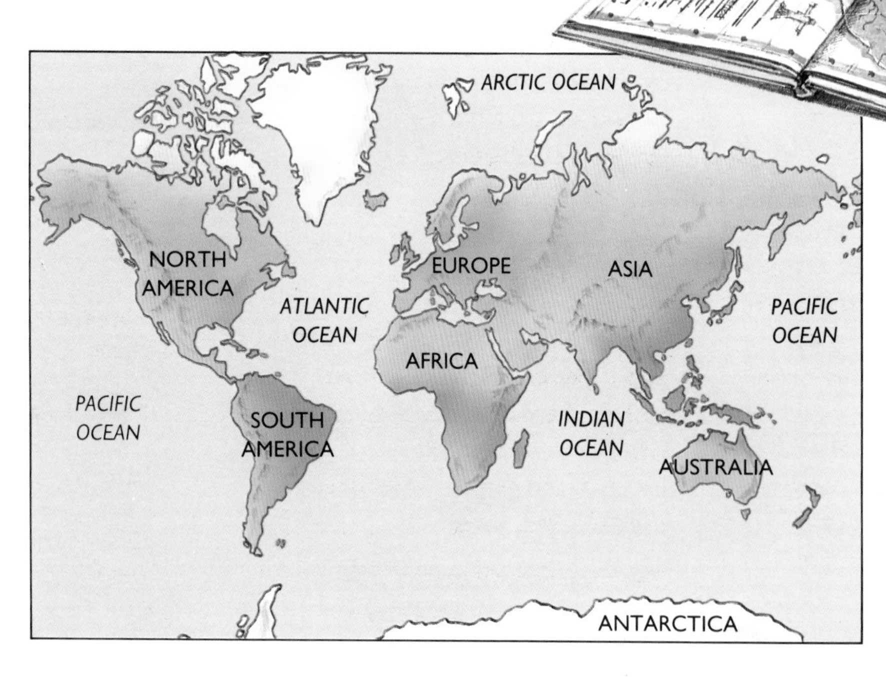


### About the maps

On the first maps each country is clearly marked in a separate colour with its capital city. The second maps are picture maps. They show the kind of animals that live on each continent, some of the plants that grow there, and the main industries. It is not possible, however, to show every spot where, for example, tigers or factories are found. There will be tigers and factories in other places besides those marked.

On the maps you will see where the biggest mountain ranges are, where the rivers flow to, what the names of the largest lakes are, as well as the names of the countries and their capital cities.

Each map has a scale. This will help you to work out how large the continent really is.

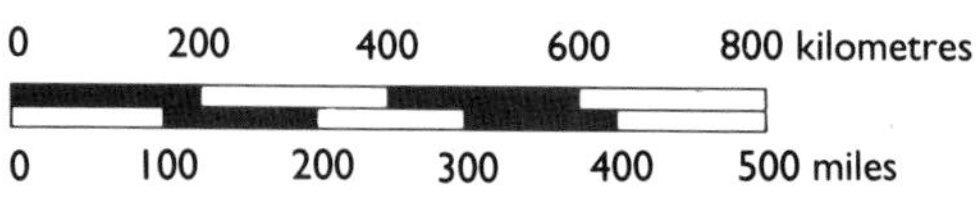


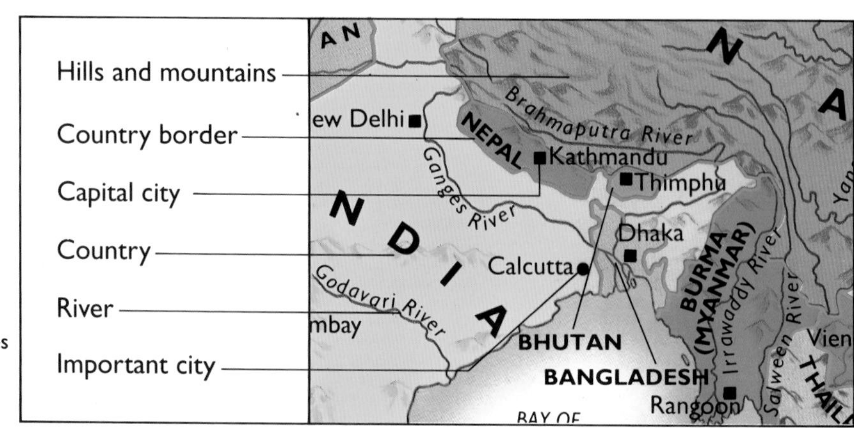

## Where is it?

If you want to find a particular place in the atlas, look for it first in the index. After the place name you will see a page number and then a number and a letter, such as **4C**. This is the grid reference. Remember it as you turn to the page. Now look for the grid number (in a red circle) at the top and bottom of the page. There is a faint blue line running on either side of them, up and down the page. Now look for the letter, on the left and right-hand sides of the page and the lines running beside these. You will find the place you are looking for in the square where the lines meet.

### MAKING A MEAL OF IT

On the picture-map pages there is a box showing a typical meal from that continent, using the food that is grown there. Of course, people eat a huge variety of things in the different parts of any continent. None the less, each continent does have its own, individual kinds of food, and its own traditional recipes based on the common ingredients that are found in the region.

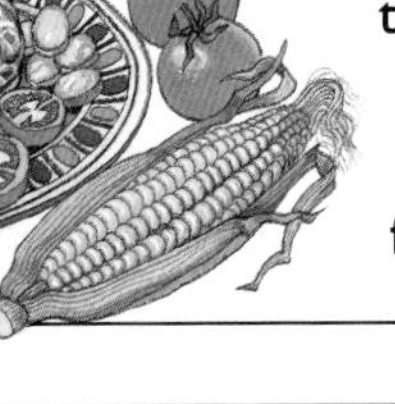

### ANSWER THAT!

On all the map pages there is a box called 'Answer That!' This asks you three questions about the map. You should be able to answer each of the questions by studying the map carefully. Look hard, and you are sure to find the solution – but some questions may require more looking than others! The correct answers to all the questions are given on page 38. Can you think of other questions to ask?

## Where it comes from and where it is made

The picture maps include a series of symbols showing you the main products and industries of a region.

A factory marks an **industry** or industrial area, and logs mark the **logging industry**. An oil rig shows where **oil** is drilled, and a flame shows **gas** production.

A mining trolley full of coal or metal, and two gemstones show where **mining** takes place.

An umbrella and suitcase show that the **tourist industry** is important in that area.

Large-scale **fishing** is represented by a trawler, and **animal farming** by two bullocks (for beef cattle), a dairy cow, a sheep and a pig.

Maize, an ear of wheat and a rice plant show where these important **cereals** are widely grown.

Various kinds of **fruit farming** are important in many parts of the world. These are shown by apples and pears, oranges and lemons, bananas, and grapes (which are also used to make wine).

**Tea, coffee and cocoa** are important and valuable crops. These are shown by tea leaves, coffee beans and cocoa pods.

**Palm trees** provide other crops such as copra from coconut palms (used to make coconut oil), dates from date palms and palm oil.

**Groundnuts** are better known as peanuts, and **sugar cane** is used to make sugar. Natural **rubber** is harvested from trees, and **cotton** comes from the fluffy seedheads of the cotton plant.

 Factory

 Logging

 Oil

 Gas

 Mining

 Gemstones

 Tourism

 Fishing

 Beef cattle

 Dairy cows

 Sheep

 Pigs

 Maize

 Wheat

 Rice

 Apples and pears

 Citrus fruits

 Bananas

 Grapes and wine

 Tea

 Coffee

 Cocoa

 Palm tree

 Groundnuts

 Sugar cane

 Rubber

 Cotton

# How maps are made

Maps are very clear and simple pictures of the world. They show us where places are, and how we might get from one place to another. Maps of the world are the result of years of work by navigators and surveyors, who have visited the places and measured the shapes of land, the heights of mountains, the courses of rivers and the position of towns and cities. In recent years, pictures from space have helped to make maps even more accurate.

One of the big problems with maps of the world is that the world is not flat, but round.

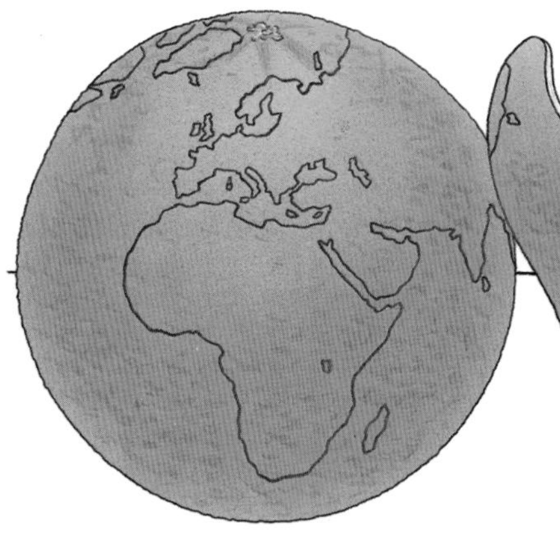

To draw a flat map of the round world we have to cheat a little. Imagine the world as an orange.

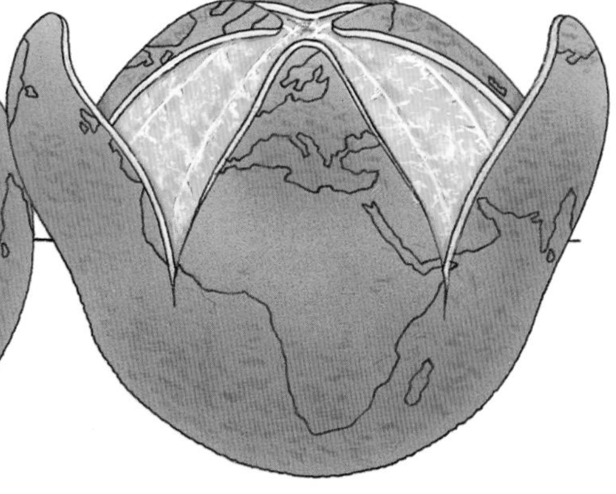

Peel the skin off the orange, into segments of equal sizes. See how the segments are oval-shaped?

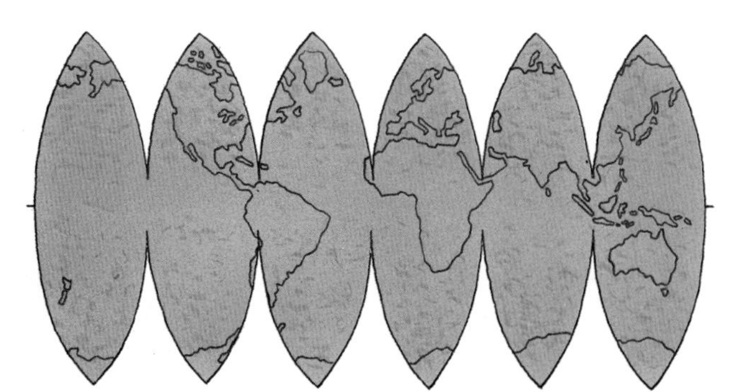

With the whole peel removed you have a true picture of the surface of the world divided into a row of oval segments.

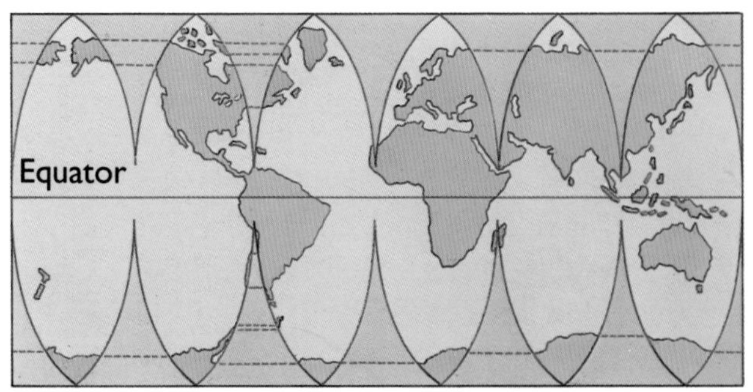


But this does not make a very helpful map. So we cheat by stretching the Earth's surface to fill in the gaps between the segments to make a rectangle.

## Map and scales

**1.** Using scale is a way of drawing places very much smaller than they are in real life, but still showing exactly where they are. If you are in Paris you can see the Eiffel Tower at its real size.

**2.** A map of the Eiffel Tower will need to be drawn smaller than real size – to a smaller scale. So, for example, every 2 centimetres on the map is equal to 150 metres of the real place or area.

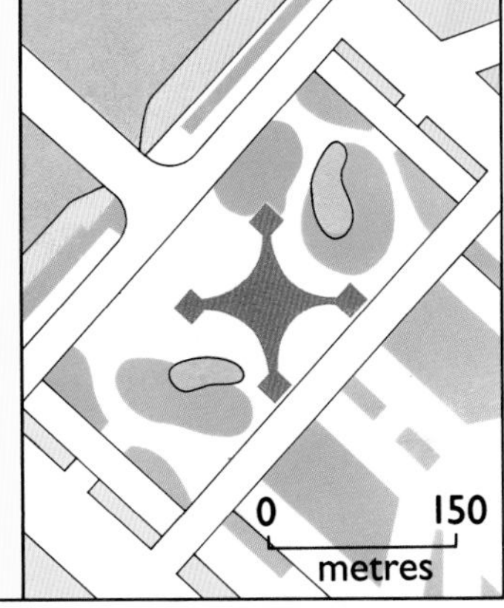


**3.** Maps can be drawn to any scale depending on what they are trying to show. A map of Paris shows the area of the city and two sizes of roads, but cannot show the Eiffel Tower in detail.

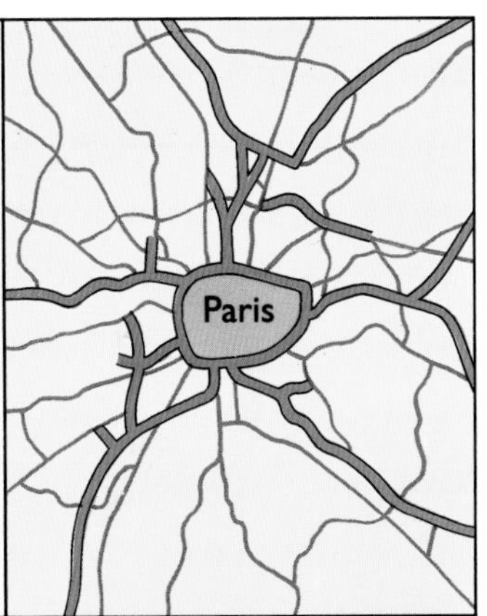


**4.** With an even smaller scale, a map will show much less detail about the city itself, but more about the country around it. A map of France will simply show where Paris is placed in the country.

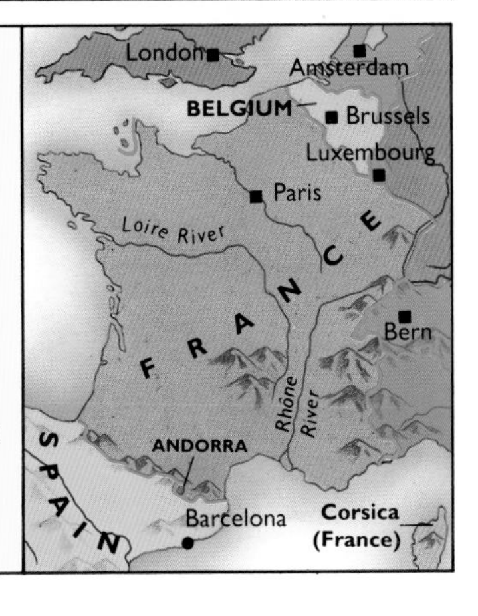


## Make your own map

Try making your own map of a place you know well, such as the area between your home and your school. Imagine how it would look from above. Draw in the streets, and show where all the main buildings are. Add any railways, parks, rivers and bridges. Keep the map as simple as possible by using symbols so that you can get more information into a small space. Could your friends use the map to find your home?

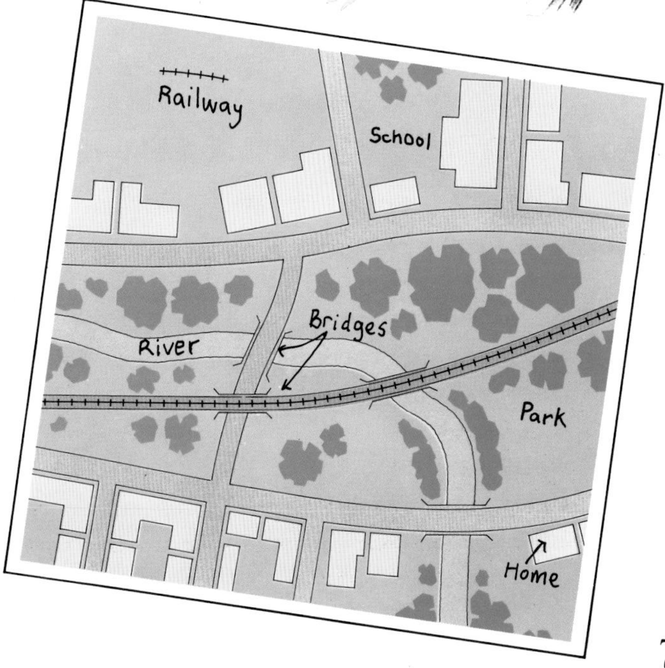

# Climate and lands

Every part of the world has its own climate or pattern of weather. It may be warm in summer, rainy in spring and very cold in winter. Or it may be hot all year round. The climate of a country depends on the shape of its land, as well as its position in the world.

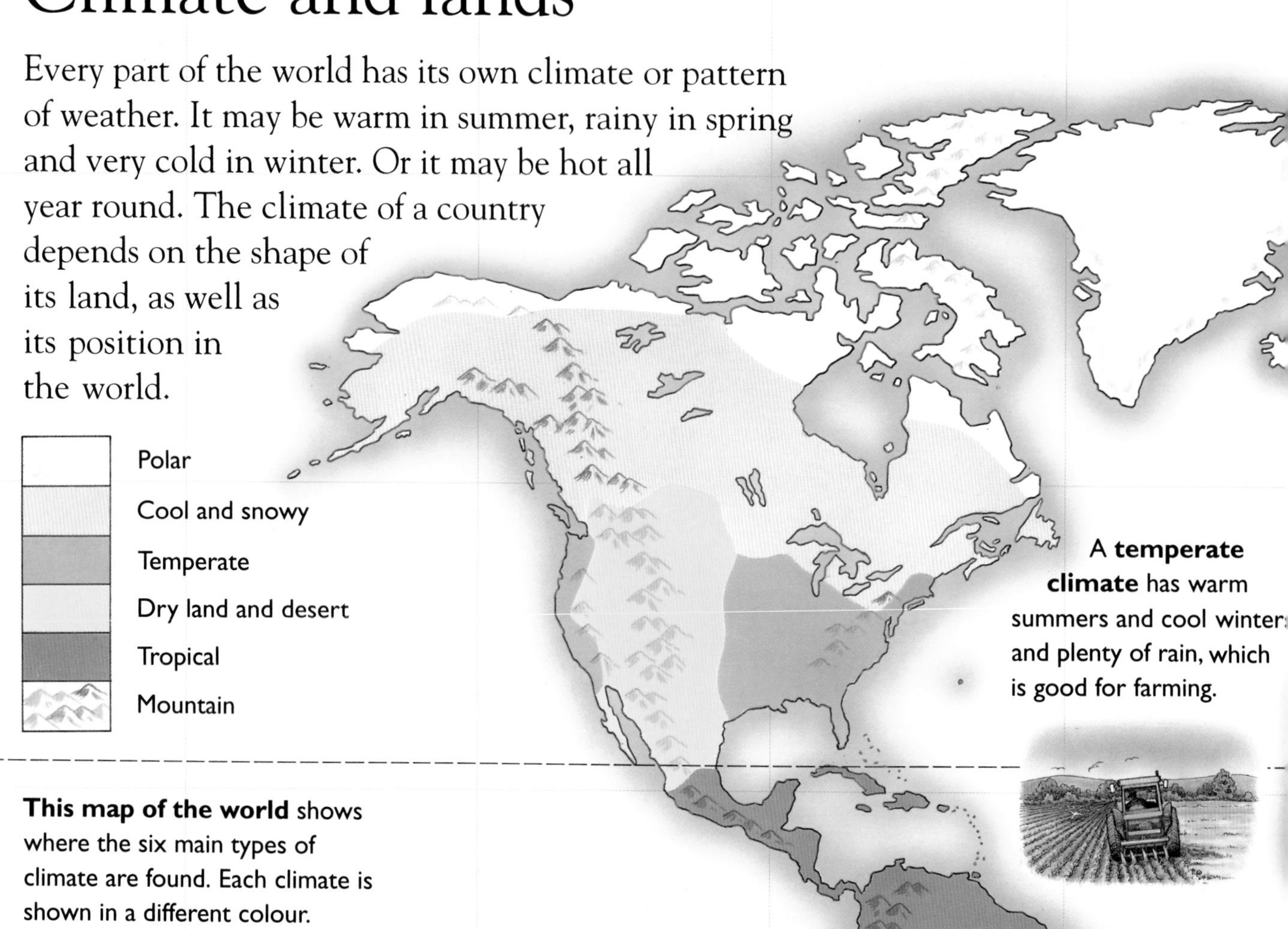


A **temperate climate** has warm summers and cool winters and plenty of rain, which is good for farming.

**This map of the world** shows where the six main types of climate are found. Each climate is shown in a different colour.

**SOME WORLD FACTS**

**Longest river** the Nile River (6,670 kilometres).
**Highest mountain** Mount Everest (8,848 metres).
**Highest waterfall** Angel Falls, Venezuela 979 metres.
**Largest country** Russia (17 million square kilometres).
**Smallest independent country** the Vatican City State, in Italy (less that half a square kilometre).
**Largest continent** Asia.
**Smallest continent** Australia.
**Largest ocean** the Pacific.

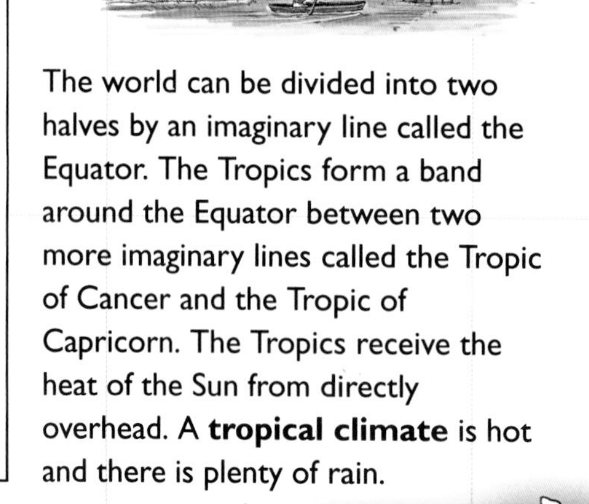

The world can be divided into two halves by an imaginary line called the Equator. The Tropics form a band around the Equator between two more imaginary lines called the Tropic of Cancer and the Tropic of Capricorn. The Tropics receive the heat of the Sun from directly overhead. A **tropical climate** is hot and there is plenty of rain.

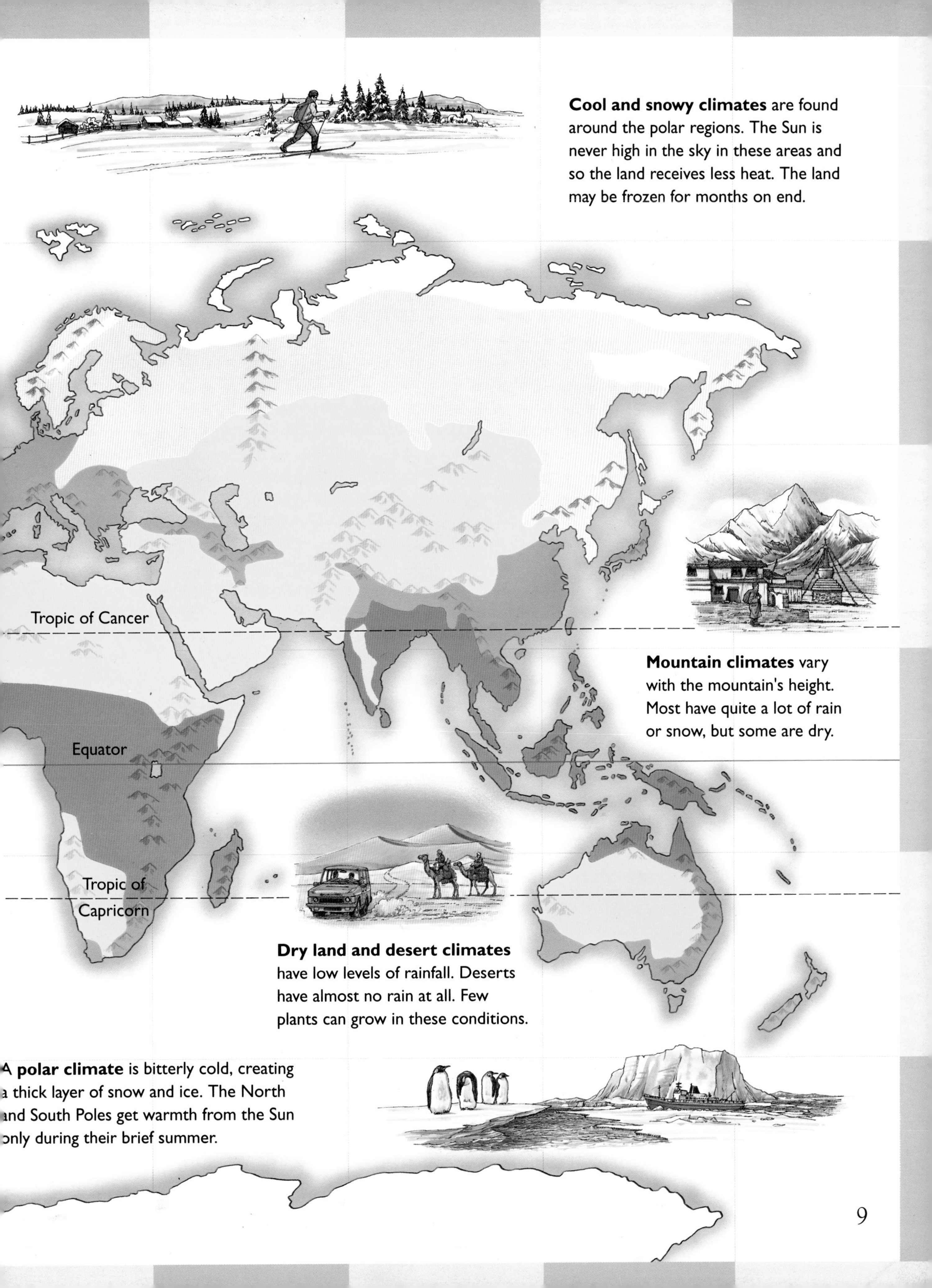


**Cool and snowy climates** are found around the polar regions. The Sun is never high in the sky in these areas and so the land receives less heat. The land may be frozen for months on end.

**Mountain climates** vary with the mountain's height. Most have quite a lot of rain or snow, but some are dry.

**Dry land and desert climates** have low levels of rainfall. Deserts have almost no rain at all. Few plants can grow in these conditions.

A **polar climate** is bitterly cold, creating a thick layer of snow and ice. The North and South Poles get warmth from the Sun only during their brief summer.

# North America

Two English-speaking countries occupy most of North America: Canada and the United States of America (or USA). The USA is one of the world's richest and most powerful countries. It is divided into 50 states, including the huge, separate state of Alaska.

To the south lies the warm Caribbean Sea, with hundreds of islands. A ribbon of land links North America to South America and contains a cluster of Spanish-speaking countries. Together these are known as Central America.

**The Inuit (or Eskimo) people** live in the very cold lands in the far north of Canada. In the past, they made houses called igloos from blocks of snow, and travelled on dog-sleds. Now they also use motorized snowmobiles.

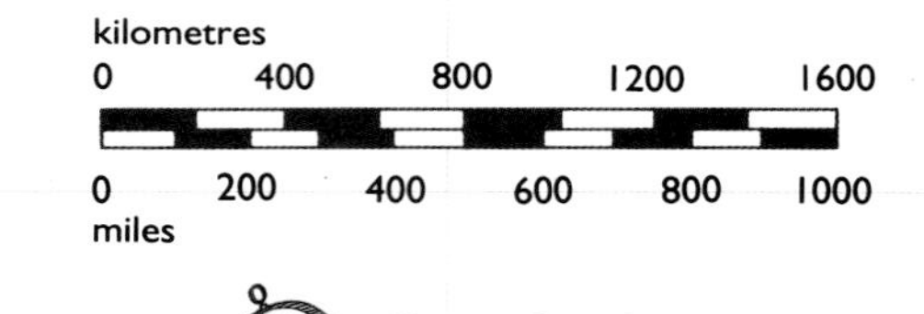


**Greenland** is the largest island in the world. Although it is close to North America, its government is linked to Denmark. Most of the land is covered with snow and ice.



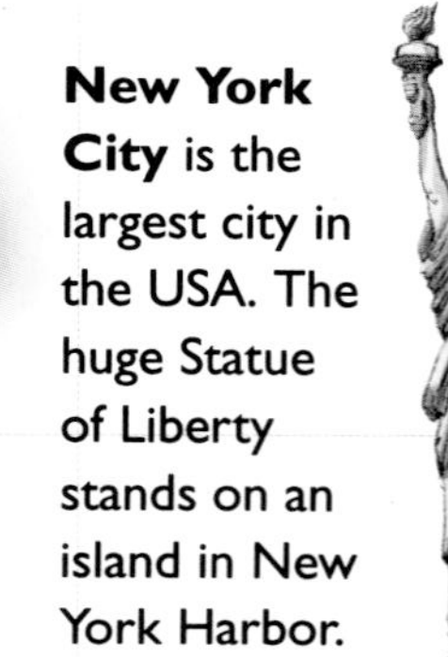

**New York City** is the largest city in the USA. The huge Statue of Liberty stands on an island in New York Harbor.

**Canada** is the second largest country in the world. The northern part is remote and empty. Most people live in the south, close to the USA.

**The Hawaiian Islands** lie about 3,800 kilometres from the west coast of the USA, in the Pacific Ocean. This group of 132 islands forms Hawaii, a state of the USA. The islands are boxed to show that they are drawn closer to the mainland of the USA than they really are.

**Washington DC** is the capital of the USA. It contains government buildings, such as the Capitol, where the US Congress meets.

## ANSWER THAT!

**1.** Which country is attached to the south of the USA?
**2.** Which is the largest island in the Caribbean Sea?
**3.** Which island is called green, but is hardly green at all?

**Mexico** is a Spanish-speaking country with volcanoes and mountains, and long, sandy beaches. Its capital, Mexico City, is one of the largest cities in the world.

**The Panama Canal** was opened in 1914. Before then, ships had to sail all the way round South America to travel between the Pacific and the Atlantic Oceans.

For the capital cities of the smaller islands, look up the country name in the index.

**St Kitts and Nevis** are two small Caribbean islands, which together form the smallest independent country in North America.

**Timber** is one of the most important products of Canada. The wood is made into planks and paper. The workers who cut down the trees are called lumberjacks.

**Beavers** live in many of the smaller rivers of North America. They cut down young trees to build dams and homes called lodges. The dams block the streams and create small lakes.

**MAKING A MEAL OF IT**

Every November, people in the USA celebrate Thanksgiving by eating a traditional meal of turkey with cranberry sauce, sweet corn and sweet potatoes, and pumpkin pie.

**Mount McKinley**, in Alaska, is the highest mountain in North America. It rises to 6,194 metres. It is surrounded by the Denali National Park. (Denali is the Native American name for Mount McKinley).

**The Great Lakes** are five huge lakes formed by the Saint Lawrence River. They lie on the border between Canada and the USA.

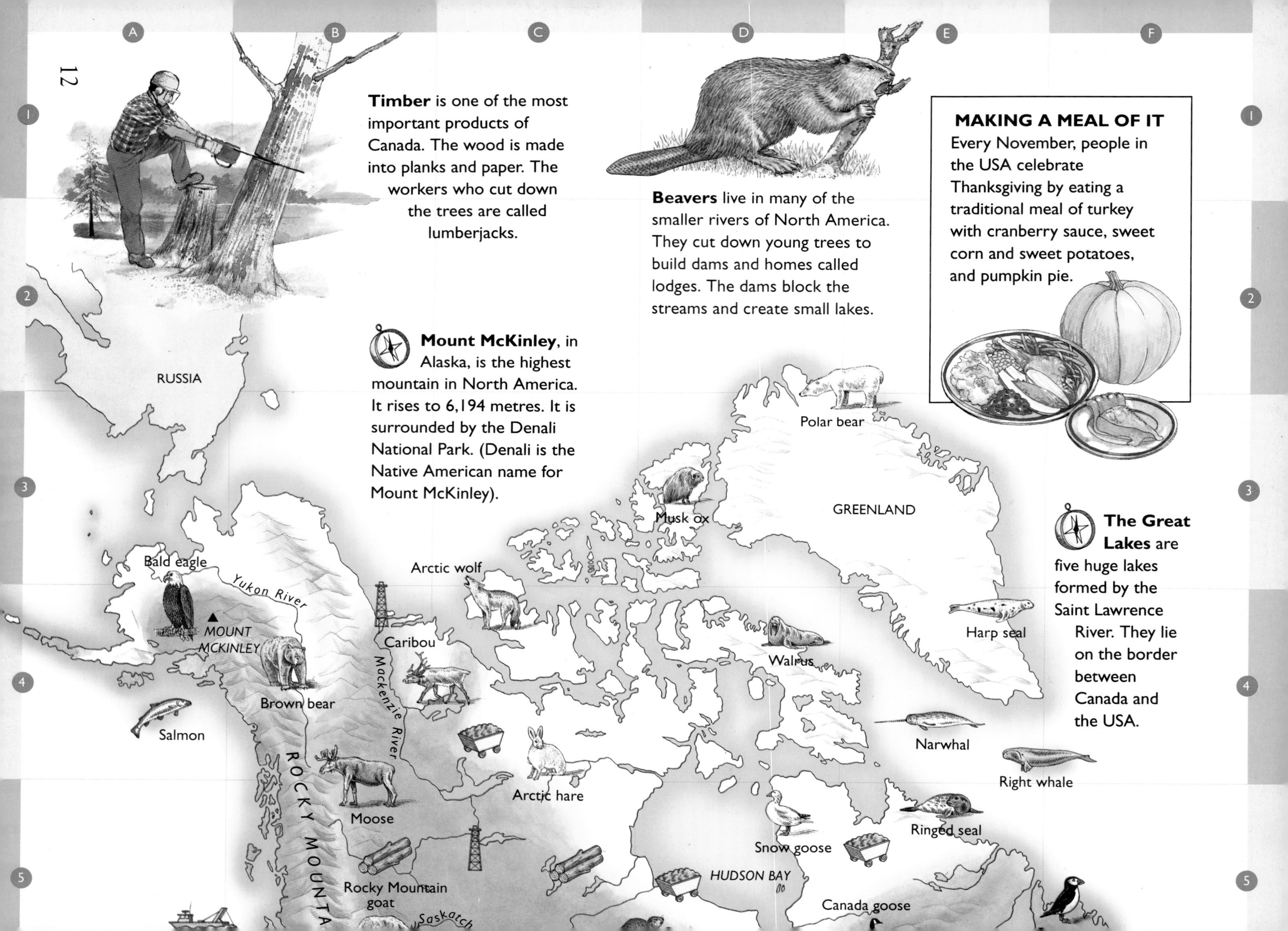

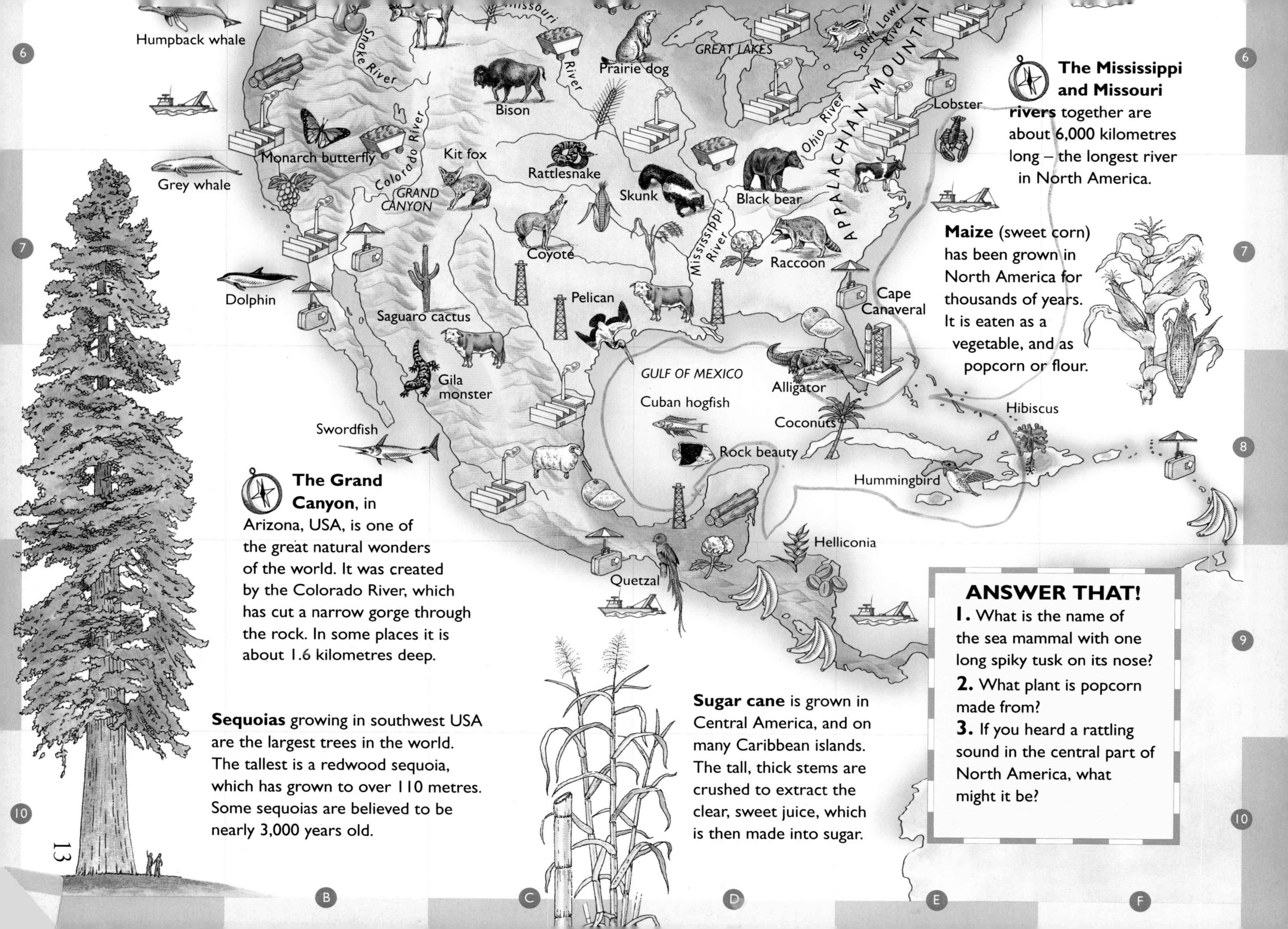


**The Mississippi and Missouri rivers** together are about 6,000 kilometres long – the longest river in North America.

**Maize** (sweet corn) has been grown in North America for thousands of years. It is eaten as a vegetable, and as popcorn or flour.

**The Grand Canyon**, in Arizona, USA, is one of the great natural wonders of the world. It was created by the Colorado River, which has cut a narrow gorge through the rock. In some places it is about 1.6 kilometres deep.

**Sequoias** growing in southwest USA are the largest trees in the world. The tallest is a redwood sequoia, which has grown to over 110 metres. Some sequoias are believed to be nearly 3,000 years old.

**Sugar cane** is grown in Central America, and on many Caribbean islands. The tall, thick stems are crushed to extract the clear, sweet juice, which is then made into sugar.

## ANSWER THAT!

**1.** What is the name of the sea mammal with one long spiky tusk on its nose?

**2.** What plant is popcorn made from?

**3.** If you heard a rattling sound in the central part of North America, what might it be?

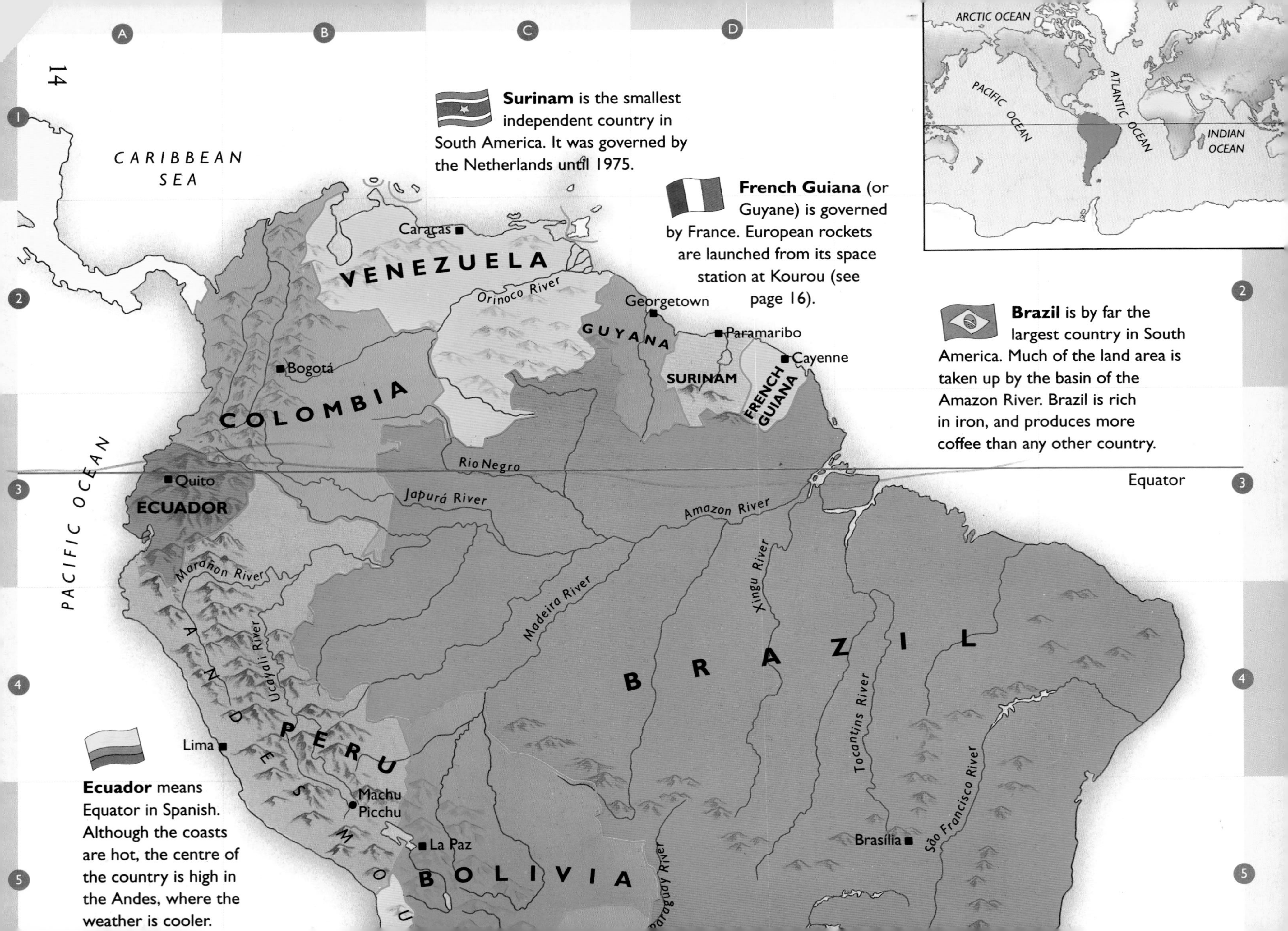


**Surinam** is the smallest independent country in South America. It was governed by the Netherlands until 1975.

**French Guiana** (or Guyane) is governed by France. European rockets are launched from its space station at Kourou (see page 16).

**Brazil** is by far the largest country in South America. Much of the land area is taken up by the basin of the Amazon River. Brazil is rich in iron, and produces more coffee than any other country.

**Ecuador** means Equator in Spanish. Although the coasts are hot, the centre of the country is high in the Andes, where the weather is cooler.

**La Paz** is the world's highest capital city, standing 3,627 metres above sea level. The air is thinner at this height, and visitors from other lower countries can feel quite breathless.

**Machu Picchu** is a ruined city of the ancient Inca people. It lies high in the mountains of Peru and remained hidden for hundreds of years before it was rediscovered in 1911.

**ANSWER THAT!**

**1.** How many countries in South America begin with the letter B?
**2.** What is the name of the longest and thinnest country in South America?
**3.** Which country has coasts on the Pacific Ocean and on the Caribbean Sea?

**Punta Arenas** is further south than any other city in the world.

**Rio de Janeiro** has a huge statue of Jesus on a hill above the city. São Paulo, to the west, is the biggest city in South America. It has a population of over 10 million.

# South America

In the very south of South America the sea is ice-cold. But the shore of the north coast is on the warm Caribbean Sea. In between are the huge tropical forests around the Amazon River in Brazil, and the vast grassy plains called the Pampas in Argentina and Uruguay. The Andes run down the western side of South America.

Originally the native peoples spoke many different languages. Then about 500 years ago, European settlers arrived and now most of the people of South America speak Spanish, except in Brazil, where the main language is Portuguese.

**The Angel Falls** is the highest waterfall in the world. The water tumbles from a height of 979 metres.

**The Amazon River** is 6,448 kilometres long (slightly shorter than the Nile River in Africa). However, it carries far more water than any other river in the world, and 60 times more than the Nile.

## ANSWER THAT!

**1.** Which South American animal likes to hang upside down from branches?
**2.** One animal likes to eat ants, which it picks up with its sticky tongue. What is its name?
**3.** Which frog can be used to make poison arrows?

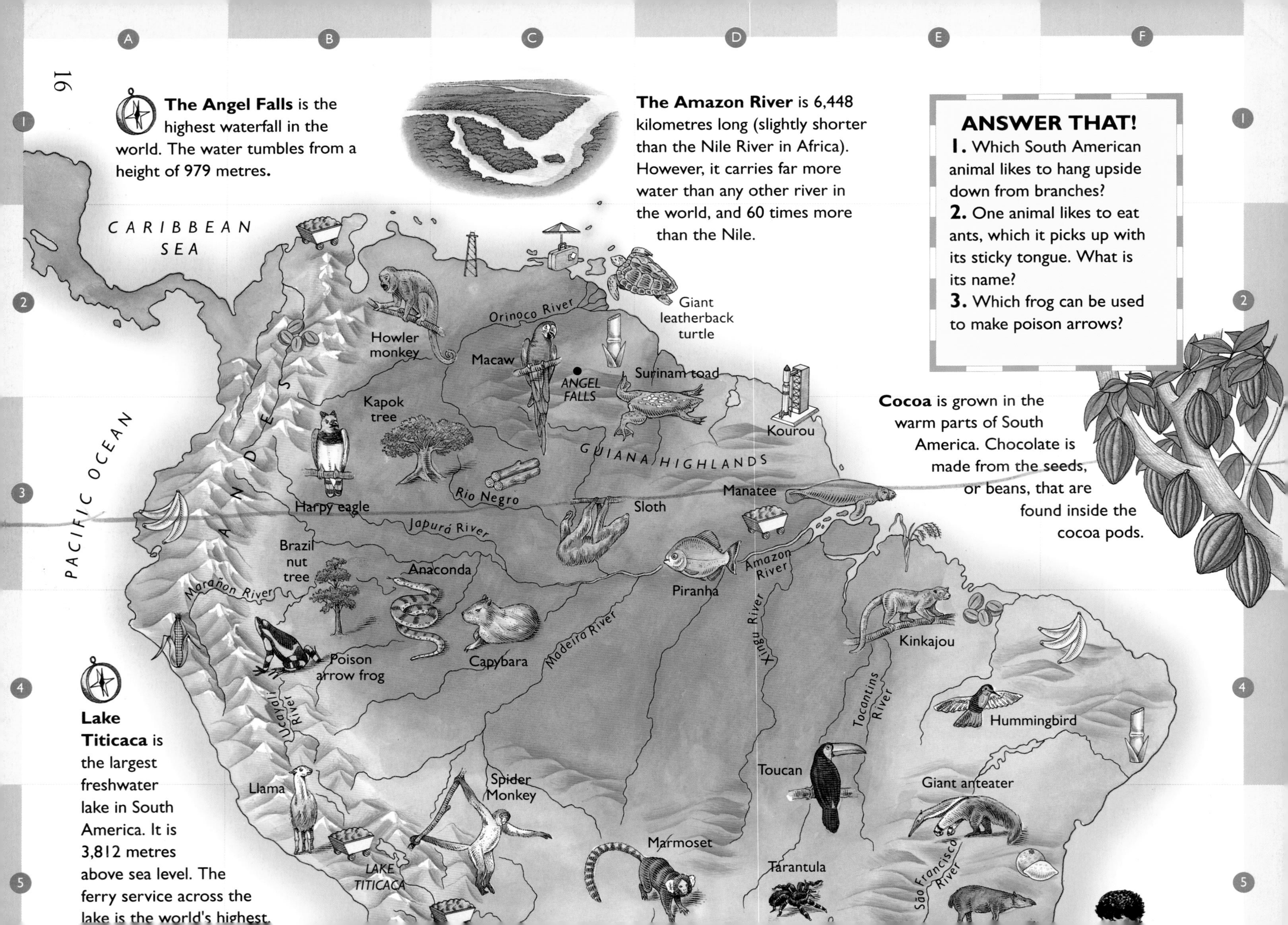


**Cocoa** is grown in the warm parts of South America. Chocolate is made from the seeds, or beans, that are found inside the cocoa pods.

**Lake Titicaca** is the largest freshwater lake in South America. It is 3,812 metres above sea level. The ferry service across the lake is the world's highest.

**The Atacama Desert** is one of the driest places on Earth. Some parts of it have gone 400 years without rain.

**Condors** are large vultures that live in the Andes. Some have a wingspan of over 3.2 metres. They feed on the bodies of dead animals.

**The Andes** form the longest mountain range in the world. They stretch for over 7,250 kilometres. The highest peak is Aconcagua, which rises to 6,959 metres.

**Football** is a favourite sport all over South America. Brazil was the first country to win the World Cup three times.

**The Pampas** covers much of Argentina and Uruguay. Large herds of beef cattle are raised on these huge grassy plains. They are looked after by cowboys called gauchos.

**Elephant seals** are the largest of all seals. They live in cold waters and breed on the shores of southern Argentina. Male elephant seals can be as much as 6 metres long.

### MAKING A MEAL OF IT

Many of our common foods come originally from South America. These include sweet corn, tomatoes and potatoes. A common meal in South America consists of beef, served with boiled rice or potatoes, tomatoes and slices of fried plantain (a fruit like a banana).

# Europe

There are more than 40 countries in Europe, and about as many languages. This is a wealthy part of the world with many old, historic cities and lots of big industries producing cars, chemicals, medicines and so on. It generally has mild weather, with plenty of rain, which is good for farming. The south of Europe, around the Mediterranean Sea, has very warm summers, while the north is cooler with long, cold and dark winters.

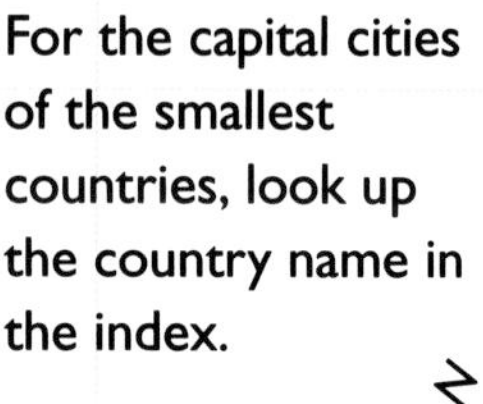

For the capital cities of the smallest countries, look up the country name in the index.

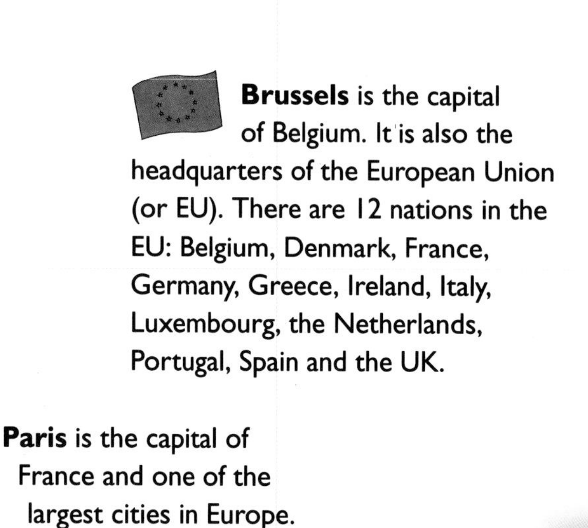

**Brussels** is the capital of Belgium. It is also the headquarters of the European Union (or EU). There are 12 nations in the EU: Belgium, Denmark, France, Germany, Greece, Ireland, Italy, Luxembourg, the Netherlands, Portugal, Spain and the UK.

**Paris** is the capital of France and one of the largest cities in Europe. Its many famous buildings include the Eiffel Tower, a huge metal tower built in 1889.

0 200 400 600 800 kilometres

0 100 200 300 400 500 miles

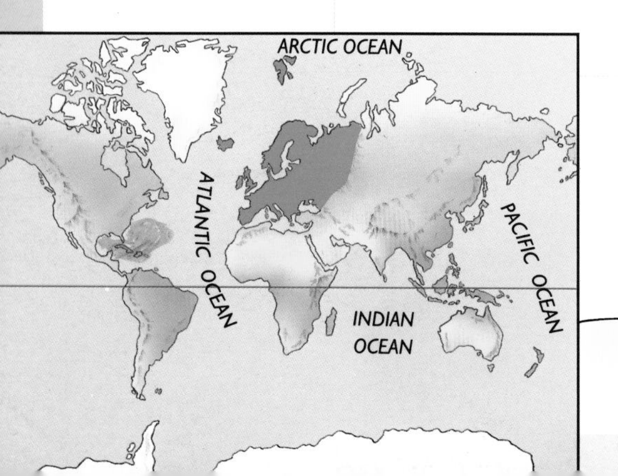


**The Vatican City State** is the smallest country in the world. It lies inside the city of Rome. The Vatican is the headquarters of the Roman Catholic Church, which is led by the Pope.

**ANSWER THAT!**

**1.** Which country earned its name because it is so icy? (Clue: it is an island).

**2.** Which city in which country is in both Europe and Asia?

**3.** Which country in Europe begins with the letter C, but does not have any sea around its borders?

**Istanbul** is the largest city in Turkey. Most of Turkey is in Asia, but a small part of it is in Europe. Istanbul lies in both Europe and Asia.

**Moscow** is the capital of Russia, and one of the largest cities in Europe. St Basil's Cathedral is so colourful that it looks as though it might be made of candy – but it is not!

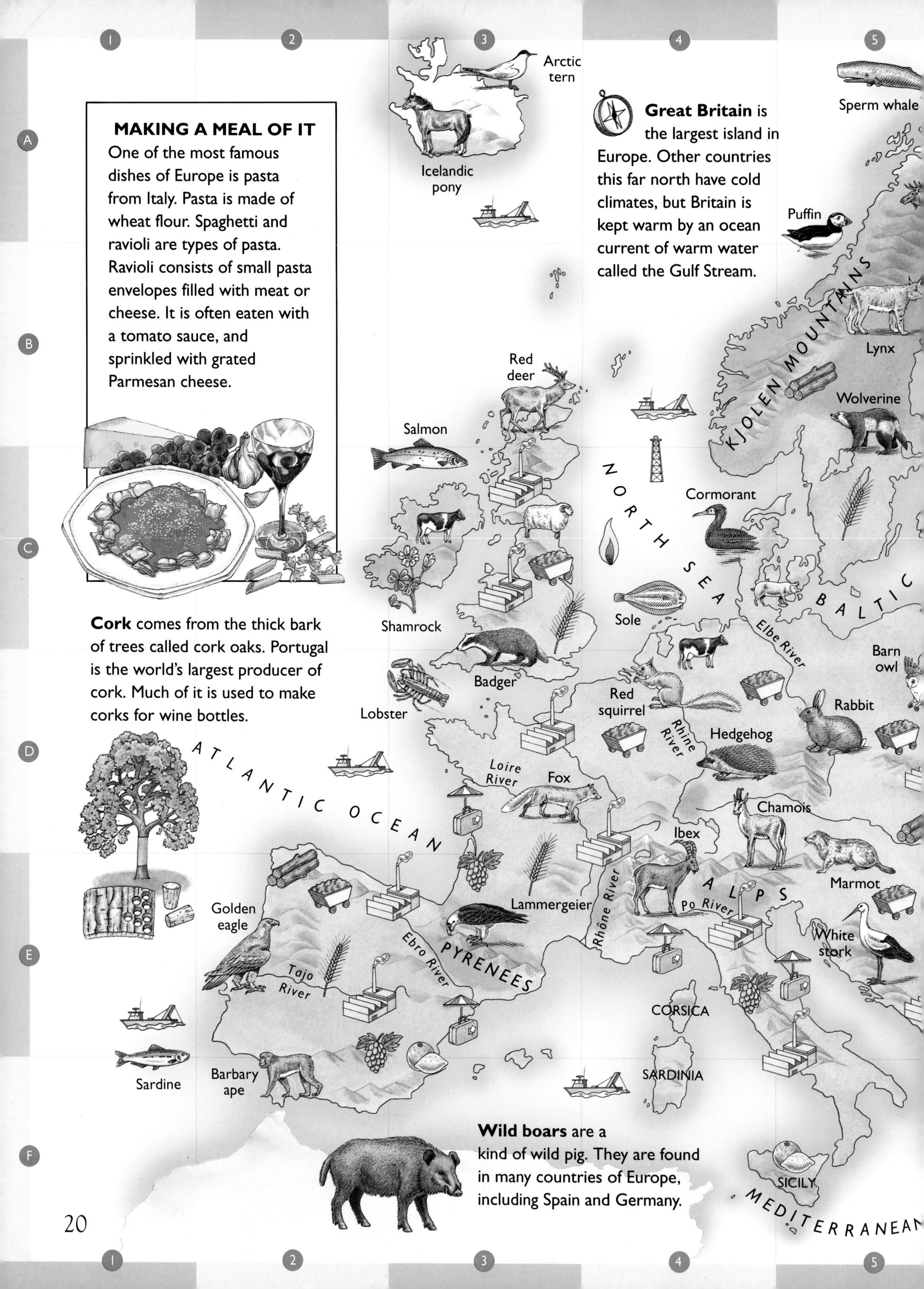


**Great Britain** is the largest island in Europe. Other countries this far north have cold climates, but Britain is kept warm by an ocean current of warm water called the Gulf Stream.

## MAKING A MEAL OF IT

One of the most famous dishes of Europe is pasta from Italy. Pasta is made of wheat flour. Spaghetti and ravioli are types of pasta. Ravioli consists of small pasta envelopes filled with meat or cheese. It is often eaten with a tomato sauce, and sprinkled with grated Parmesan cheese.

**Cork** comes from the thick bark of trees called cork oaks. Portugal is the world's largest producer of cork. Much of it is used to make corks for wine bottles.

**Wild boars** are a kind of wild pig. They are found in many countries of Europe, including Spain and Germany.

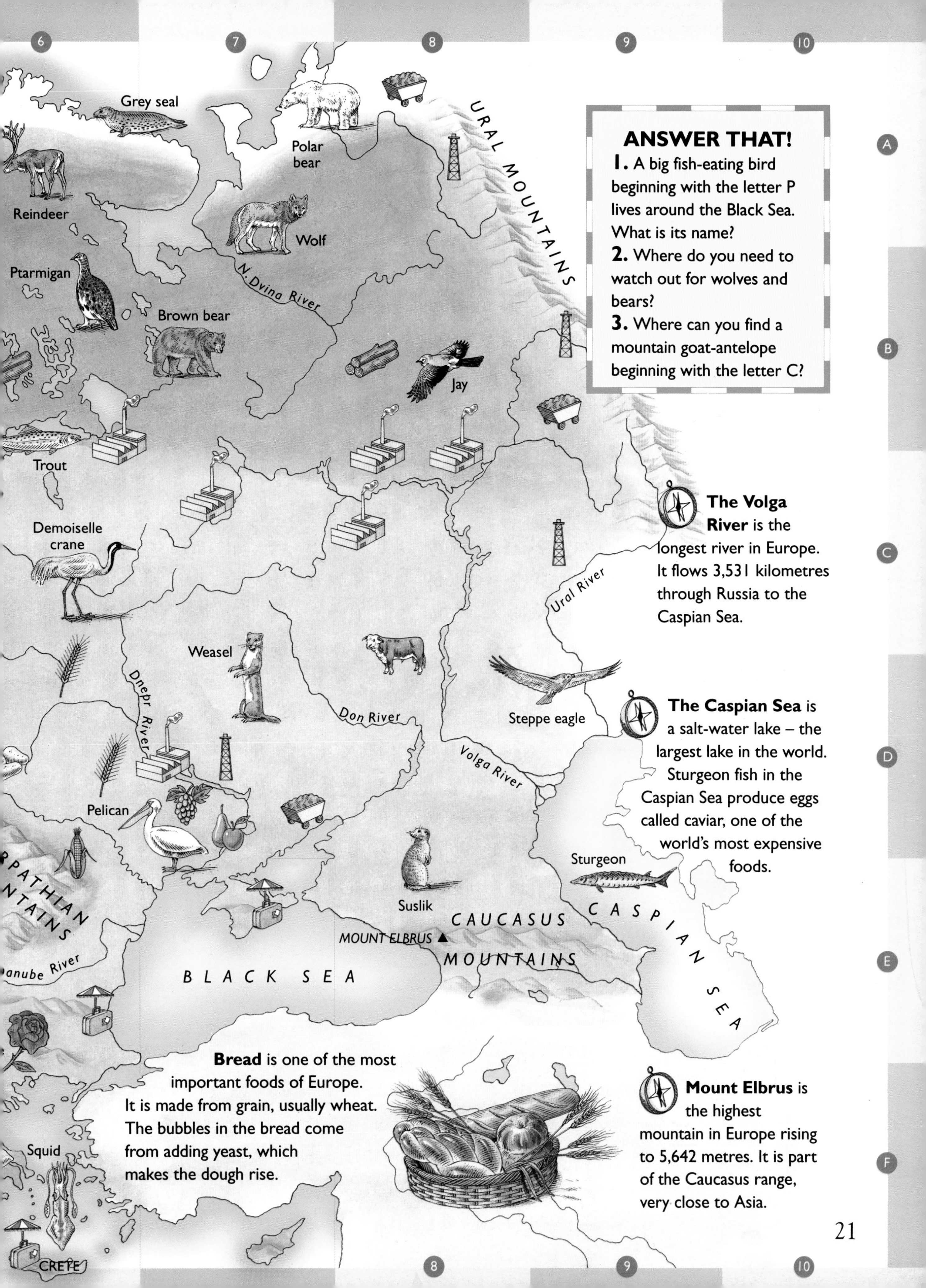


## ANSWER THAT!

**1.** A big fish-eating bird beginning with the letter P lives around the Black Sea. What is its name?

**2.** Where do you need to watch out for wolves and bears?

**3.** Where can you find a mountain goat-antelope beginning with the letter C?

**The Volga River** is the longest river in Europe. It flows 3,531 kilometres through Russia to the Caspian Sea.

**The Caspian Sea** is a salt-water lake – the largest lake in the world. Sturgeon fish in the Caspian Sea produce eggs called caviar, one of the world's most expensive foods.

**Bread** is one of the most important foods of Europe. It is made from grain, usually wheat. The bubbles in the bread come from adding yeast, which makes the dough rise.

**Mount Elbrus** is the highest mountain in Europe rising to 5,642 metres. It is part of the Caucasus range, very close to Asia.

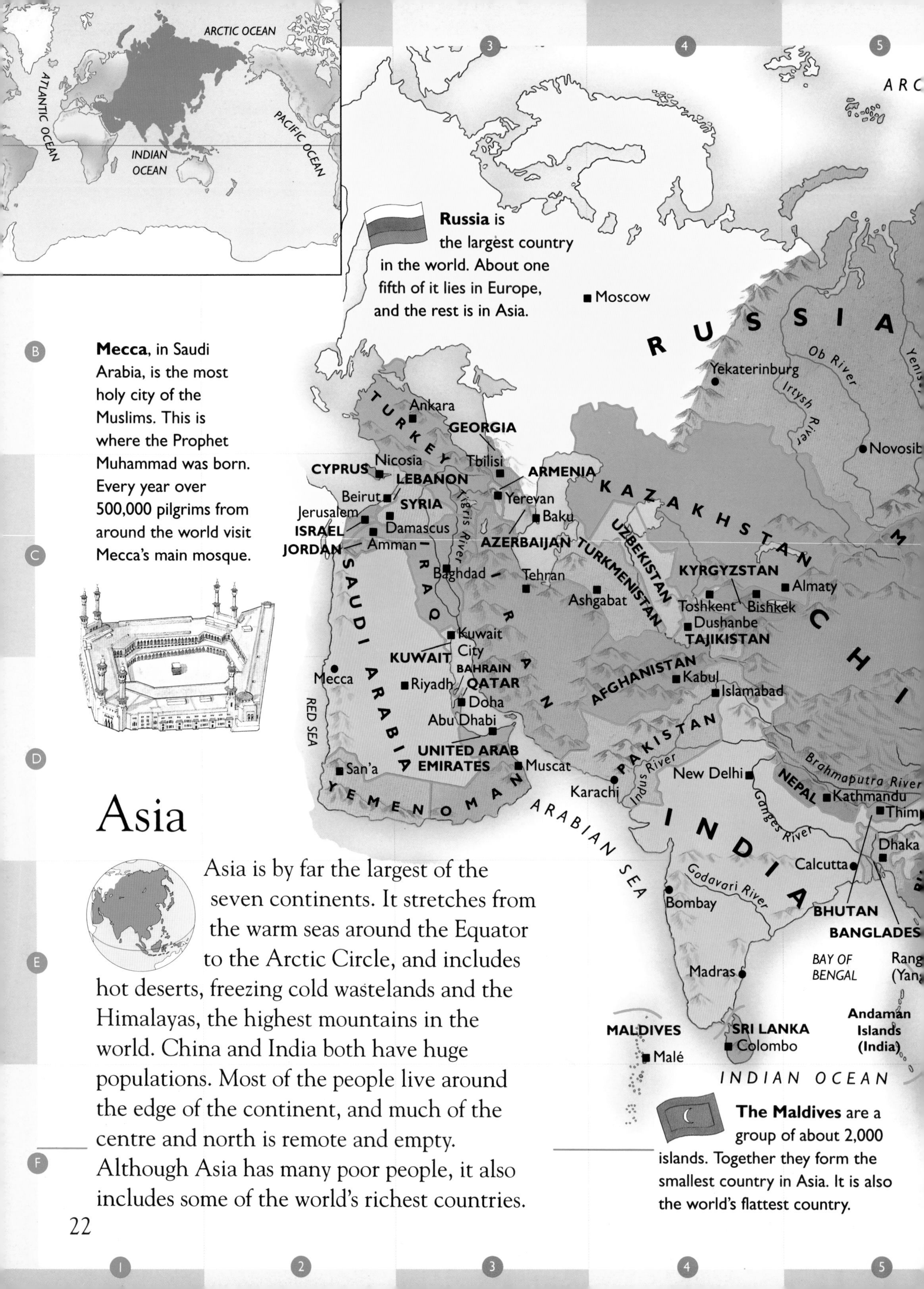


**Russia** is the largest country in the world. About one fifth of it lies in Europe, and the rest is in Asia.

**Mecca**, in Saudi Arabia, is the most holy city of the Muslims. This is where the Prophet Muhammad was born. Every year over 500,000 pilgrims from around the world visit Mecca's main mosque.

# Asia

Asia is by far the largest of the seven continents. It stretches from the warm seas around the Equator to the Arctic Circle, and includes hot deserts, freezing cold wastelands and the Himalayas, the highest mountains in the world. China and India both have huge populations. Most of the people live around the edge of the continent, and much of the centre and north is remote and empty. Although Asia has many poor people, it also includes some of the world's richest countries.

**The Maldives** are a group of about 2,000 islands. Together they form the smallest country in Asia. It is also the world's flattest country.

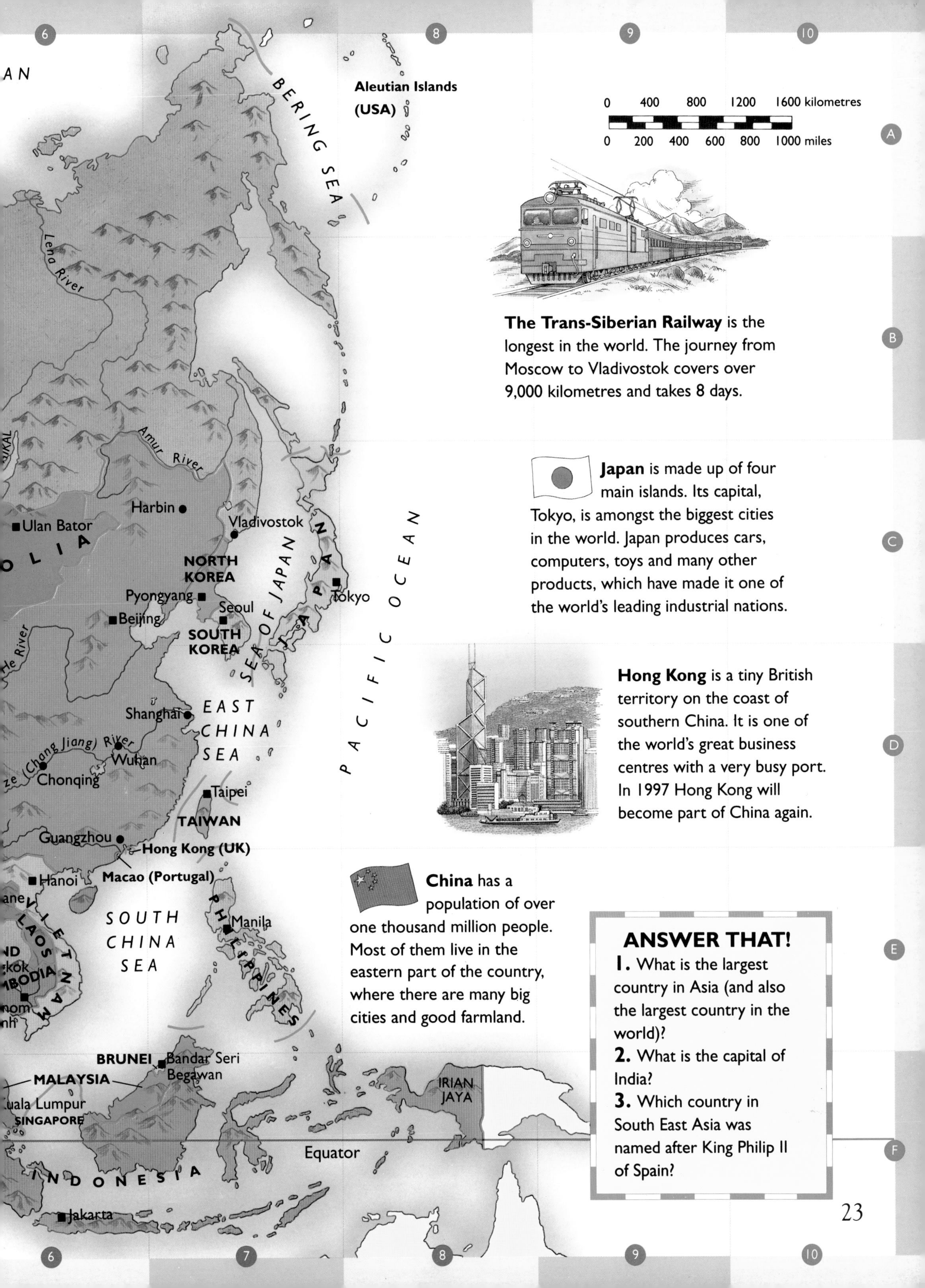


**The Trans-Siberian Railway** is the longest in the world. The journey from Moscow to Vladivostok covers over 9,000 kilometres and takes 8 days.

**Japan** is made up of four main islands. Its capital, Tokyo, is amongst the biggest cities in the world. Japan produces cars, computers, toys and many other products, which have made it one of the world's leading industrial nations.

**Hong Kong** is a tiny British territory on the coast of southern China. It is one of the world's great business centres with a very busy port. In 1997 Hong Kong will become part of China again.

**China** has a population of over one thousand million people. Most of them live in the eastern part of the country, where there are many big cities and good farmland.

## ANSWER THAT!

**1.** What is the largest country in Asia (and also the largest country in the world)?
**2.** What is the capital of India?
**3.** Which country in South East Asia was named after King Philip II of Spain?

## ANSWER THAT!

**1.** What is the proper name for a camel with two humps?
**2.** In which country can you find tigers?
**3.** Most rhinoceroses live in Africa, but there are small numbers in Asia as well. Where might you find one?

**Siberia** is a huge, cold region which covers most of Asian Russia. There are mountains and forests, and vast frozen wastes – and very few people.

**The Arabian Peninsula** is almost entirely hot, dry desert. Most of the peninsula is occupied by Saudi Arabia, which has no rivers at all.

**Oil** is one of the main products of the Middle East, the south-western part of Asia. The oil comes from wells under the ground. It is made into petrol and other products, such as tarmac and plastics.

**Mount Everest**, in the Himalayas, rises to 8,848 metres and is the highest mountain in the world. It was first climbed in 1953. All ten of the world's highest mountains are in the Himalayas.

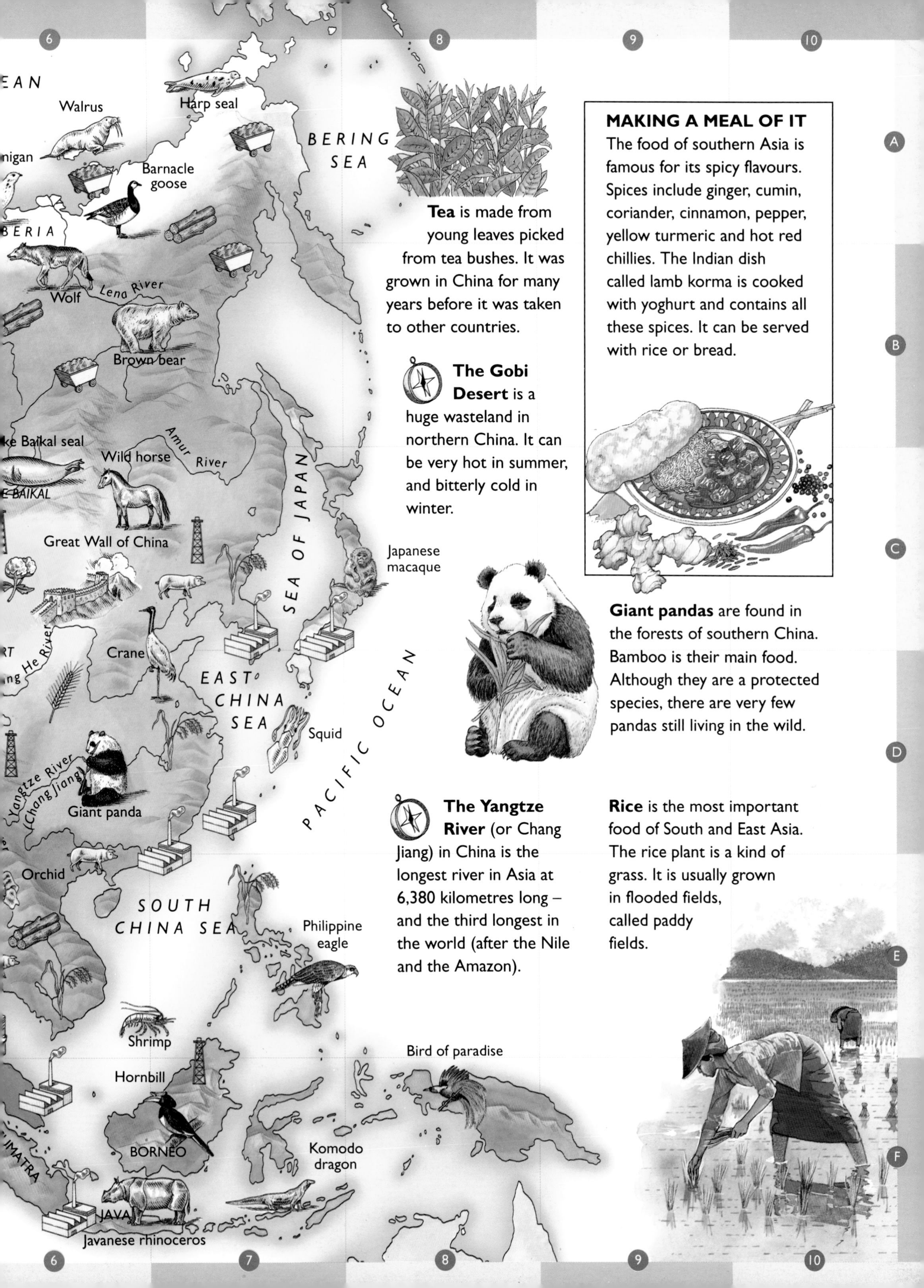


**Tea** is made from young leaves picked from tea bushes. It was grown in China for many years before it was taken to other countries.

**The Gobi Desert** is a huge wasteland in northern China. It can be very hot in summer, and bitterly cold in winter.

## MAKING A MEAL OF IT

The food of southern Asia is famous for its spicy flavours. Spices include ginger, cumin, coriander, cinnamon, pepper, yellow turmeric and hot red chillies. The Indian dish called lamb korma is cooked with yoghurt and contains all these spices. It can be served with rice or bread.

**Giant pandas** are found in the forests of southern China. Bamboo is their main food. Although they are a protected species, there are very few pandas still living in the wild.

**The Yangtze River** (or Chang Jiang) in China is the longest river in Asia at 6,380 kilometres long – and the third longest in the world (after the Nile and the Amazon).

**Rice** is the most important food of South and East Asia. The rice plant is a kind of grass. It is usually grown in flooded fields, called paddy fields.

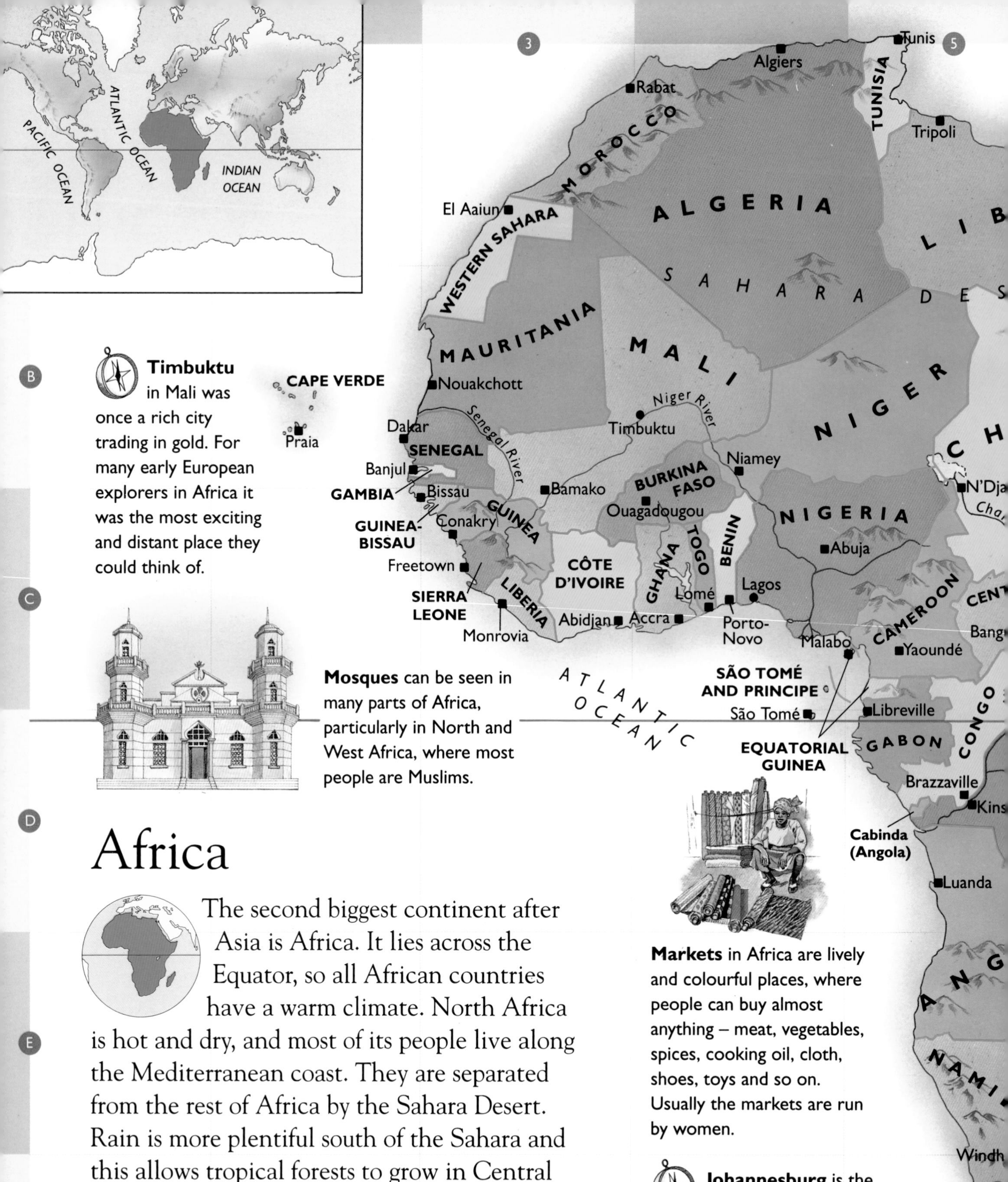


**Timbuktu** in Mali was once a rich city trading in gold. For many early European explorers in Africa it was the most exciting and distant place they could think of.

**Mosques** can be seen in many parts of Africa, particularly in North and West Africa, where most people are Muslims.

**Markets** in Africa are lively and colourful places, where people can buy almost anything – meat, vegetables, spices, cooking oil, cloth, shoes, toys and so on. Usually the markets are run by women.

**Johannesburg** is the largest city in South Africa. It developed as the centre for the goldmining industry. South Africa is the world's largest producer of gold.

# Africa

The second biggest continent after Asia is Africa. It lies across the Equator, so all African countries have a warm climate. North Africa is hot and dry, and most of its people live along the Mediterranean coast. They are separated from the rest of Africa by the Sahara Desert. Rain is more plentiful south of the Sahara and this allows tropical forests to grow in Central Africa. East Africa has drier grasslands. Many African countries are rich in diamonds, gold, and other metals. But in some areas the people are very poor and do not have enough to eat.

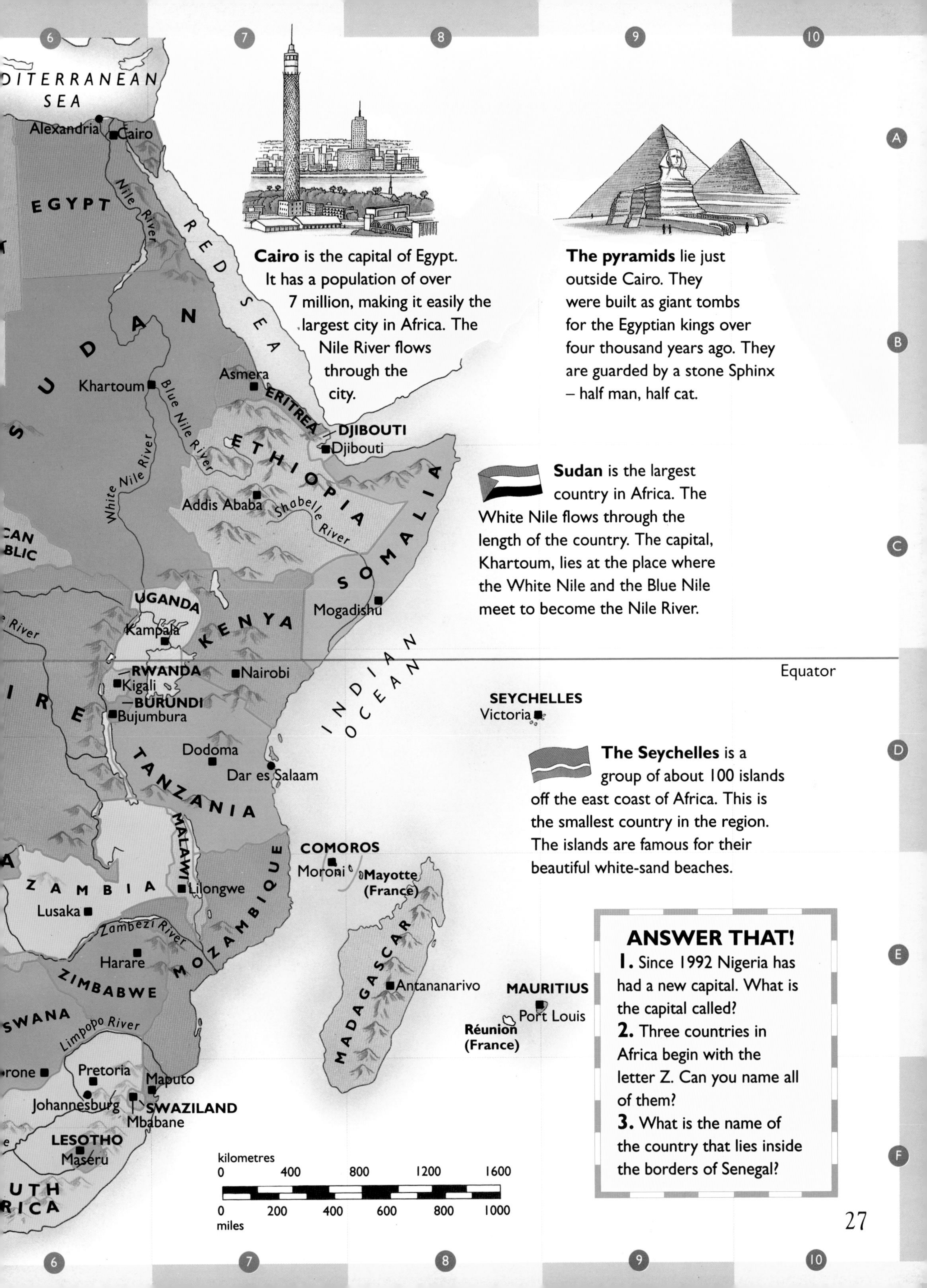


**Cairo** is the capital of Egypt. It has a population of over 7 million, making it easily the largest city in Africa. The Nile River flows through the city.

**The pyramids** lie just outside Cairo. They were built as giant tombs for the Egyptian kings over four thousand years ago. They are guarded by a stone Sphinx – half man, half cat.

**Sudan** is the largest country in Africa. The White Nile flows through the length of the country. The capital, Khartoum, lies at the place where the White Nile and the Blue Nile meet to become the Nile River.

**The Seychelles** is a group of about 100 islands off the east coast of Africa. This is the smallest country in the region. The islands are famous for their beautiful white-sand beaches.

## ANSWER THAT!

**1.** Since 1992 Nigeria has had a new capital. What is the capital called?

**2.** Three countries in Africa begin with the letter Z. Can you name all of them?

**3.** What is the name of the country that lies inside the borders of Senegal?

## MAKING A MEAL OF IT

African cookery varies from region to region. In North Africa, the most famous dish is couscous – fluffy grains of steamed wheat. In West Africa, meat stews are often cooked with a peanut sauce spiced with dried shrimps. (Peanuts are also called groundnuts.) The stews are eaten with sliced root vegetables, such as yams.

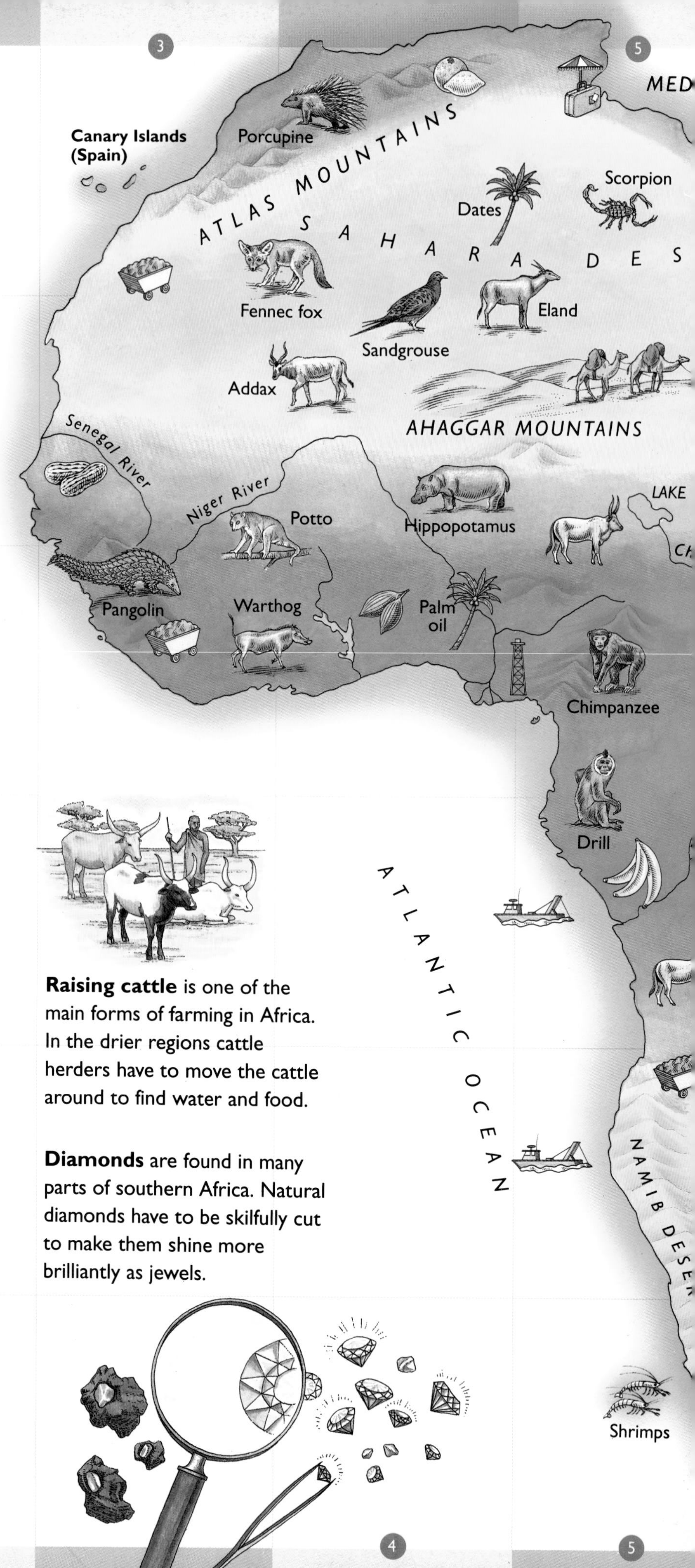


**The Sahara Desert** is the largest desert in the world. Much of it is covered by huge sand dunes, but some parts have high, rocky mountains. Camels are used to carry goods and people in desert areas.

**Raising cattle** is one of the main forms of farming in Africa. In the drier regions cattle herders have to move the cattle around to find water and food.

**Diamonds** are found in many parts of southern Africa. Natural diamonds have to be skilfully cut to make them shine more brilliantly as jewels.

## ANSWER THAT!

**1.** What is the name of the lizard from Madagascar that can change colour to match its background?
**2.** If you wanted to cross the Sahara Desert, what animal would you take to carry your baggage?
**3.** Which animal's name begins with two A's?

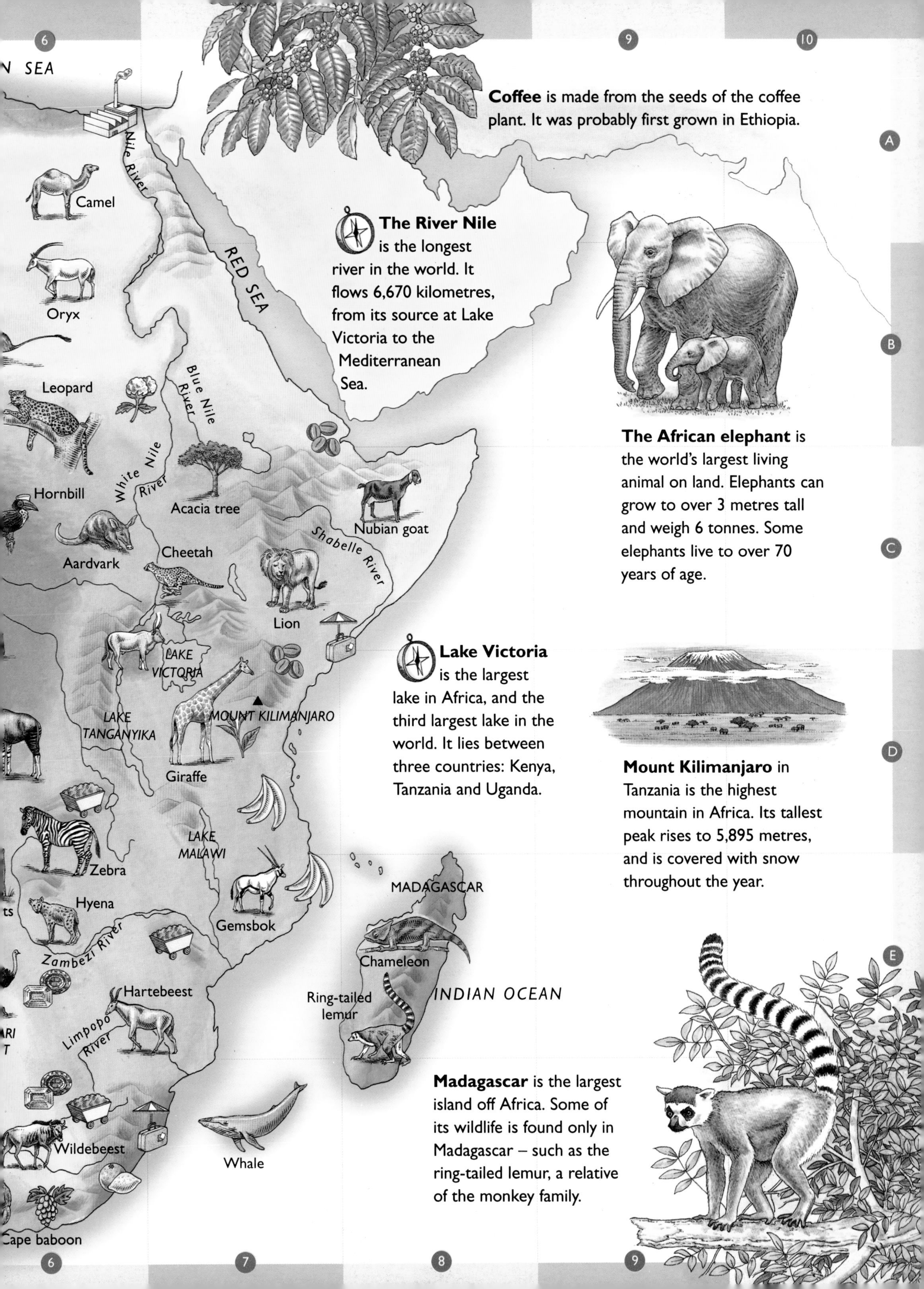


**Coffee** is made from the seeds of the coffee plant. It was probably first grown in Ethiopia.

**The River Nile** is the longest river in the world. It flows 6,670 kilometres, from its source at Lake Victoria to the Mediterranean Sea.

**The African elephant** is the world's largest living animal on land. Elephants can grow to over 3 metres tall and weigh 6 tonnes. Some elephants live to over 70 years of age.

**Lake Victoria** is the largest lake in Africa, and the third largest lake in the world. It lies between three countries: Kenya, Tanzania and Uganda.

**Mount Kilimanjaro** in Tanzania is the highest mountain in Africa. Its tallest peak rises to 5,895 metres, and is covered with snow throughout the year.

**Madagascar** is the largest island off Africa. Some of its wildlife is found only in Madagascar – such as the ring-tailed lemur, a relative of the monkey family.

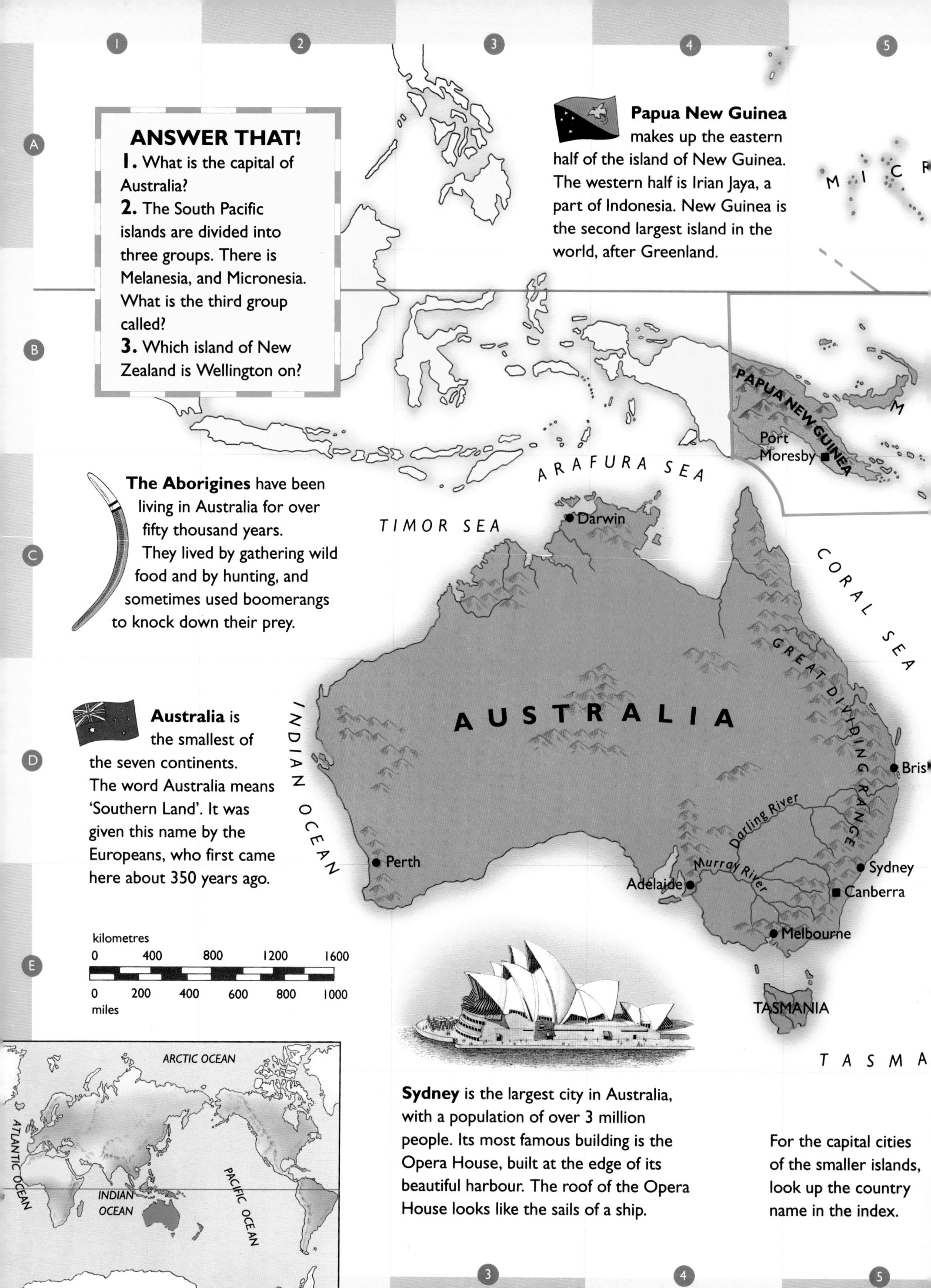


## ANSWER THAT!

**1.** What is the capital of Australia?
**2.** The South Pacific islands are divided into three groups. There is Melanesia, and Micronesia. What is the third group called?
**3.** Which island of New Zealand is Wellington on?

**Papua New Guinea** makes up the eastern half of the island of New Guinea. The western half is Irian Jaya, a part of Indonesia. New Guinea is the second largest island in the world, after Greenland.

**The Aborigines** have been living in Australia for over fifty thousand years. They lived by gathering wild food and by hunting, and sometimes used boomerangs to knock down their prey.

**Australia** is the smallest of the seven continents. The word Australia means 'Southern Land'. It was given this name by the Europeans, who first came here about 350 years ago.

**Sydney** is the largest city in Australia, with a population of over 3 million people. Its most famous building is the Opera House, built at the edge of its beautiful harbour. The roof of the Opera House looks like the sails of a ship.

For the capital cities of the smaller islands, look up the country name in the index.

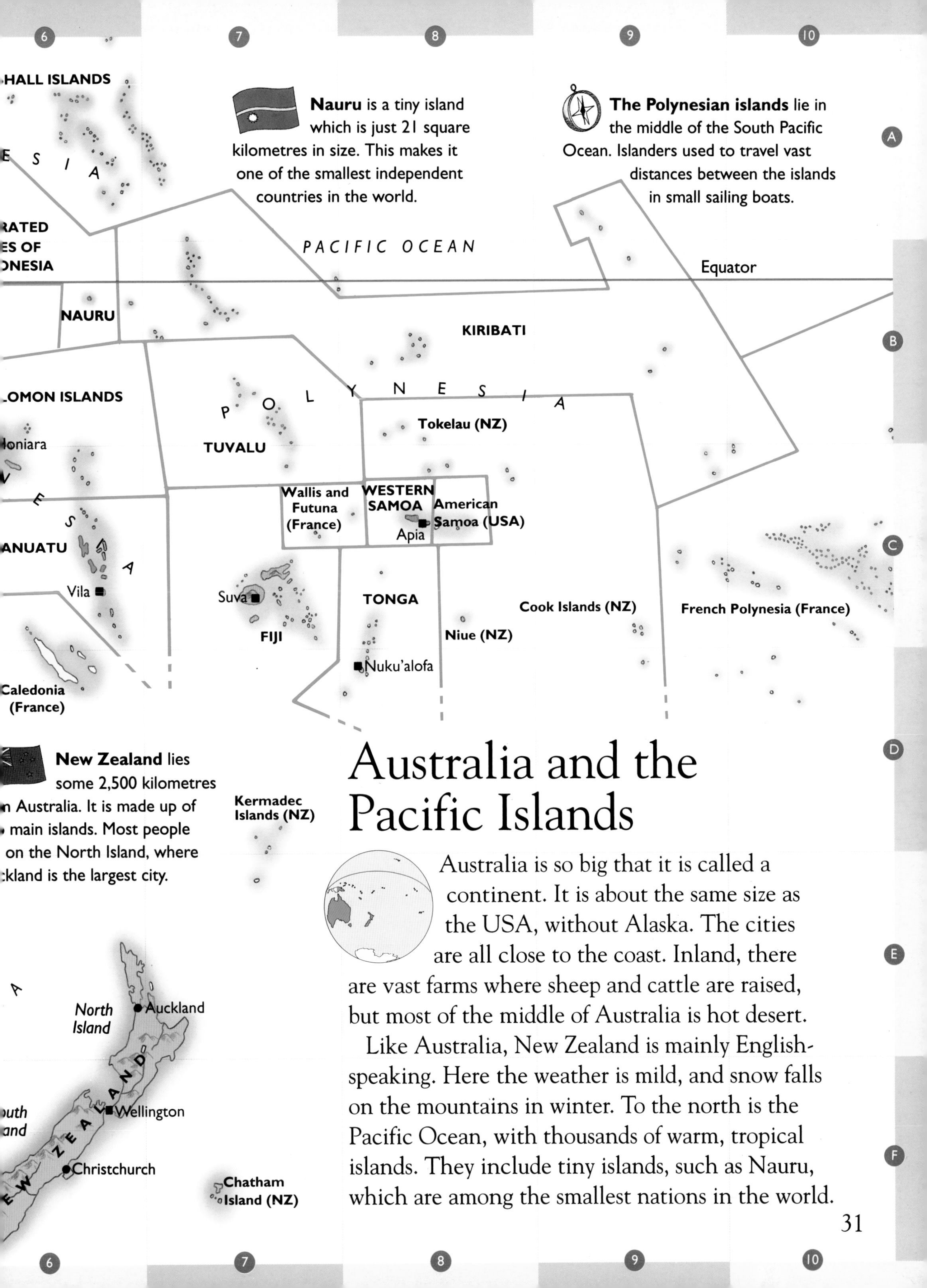


**Nauru** is a tiny island which is just 21 square kilometres in size. This makes it one of the smallest independent countries in the world.

**The Polynesian islands** lie in the middle of the South Pacific Ocean. Islanders used to travel vast distances between the islands in small sailing boats.

**New Zealand** lies some 2,500 kilometres n Australia. It is made up of main islands. Most people on the North Island, where :kland is the largest city.

# Australia and the Pacific Islands

Australia is so big that it is called a continent. It is about the same size as the USA, without Alaska. The cities are all close to the coast. Inland, there are vast farms where sheep and cattle are raised, but most of the middle of Australia is hot desert.

Like Australia, New Zealand is mainly English-speaking. Here the weather is mild, and snow falls on the mountains in winter. To the north is the Pacific Ocean, with thousands of warm, tropical islands. They include tiny islands, such as Nauru, which are among the smallest nations in the world.

## ANSWER THAT!

**1.** What colour is the famous swan of Western Australia?
**2.** What is the name of the rock in the centre of Australia?
**3.** New Zealand has two birds whose names begin with K. Neither of them can fly. What are they?

**Mount Wilhelm** is the highest mountain in the region, rising to 4,509 metres. Mount Cook, in New Zealand, is another high mountain, at 3,764 metres.

**Kangaroos** are marsupials – animals which carry their young in a pouch.

**The Darling River** flows into the Murray River in southern Australia to form the longest river of the region. It is 3,750 kilometres long.

**Sheep** are important farm animals in both Australia and New Zealand. Some of the sheep and cattle stations in Australia are as big as the country of Belgium. And there are about 18 times more sheep in New Zealand than there are people. Wool is sheared from the sheep to make cloth.

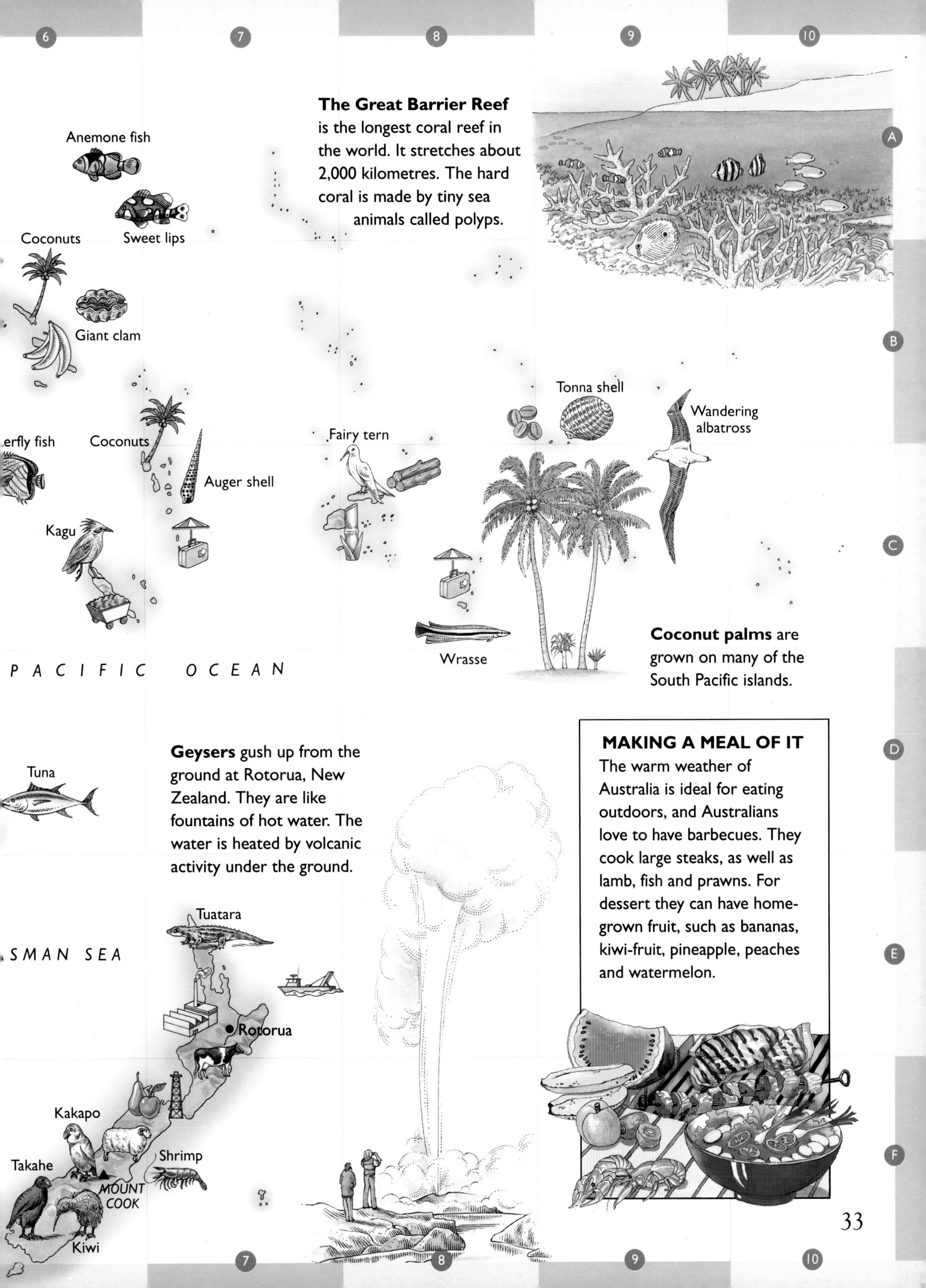


**The Great Barrier Reef** is the longest coral reef in the world. It stretches about 2,000 kilometres. The hard coral is made by tiny sea animals called polyps.

**Coconut palms** are grown on many of the South Pacific islands.

**Geysers** gush up from the ground at Rotorua, New Zealand. They are like fountains of hot water. The water is heated by volcanic activity under the ground.

## MAKING A MEAL OF IT

The warm weather of Australia is ideal for eating outdoors, and Australians love to have barbecues. They cook large steaks, as well as lamb, fish and prawns. For dessert they can have home-grown fruit, such as bananas, kiwi-fruit, pineapple, peaches and watermelon.

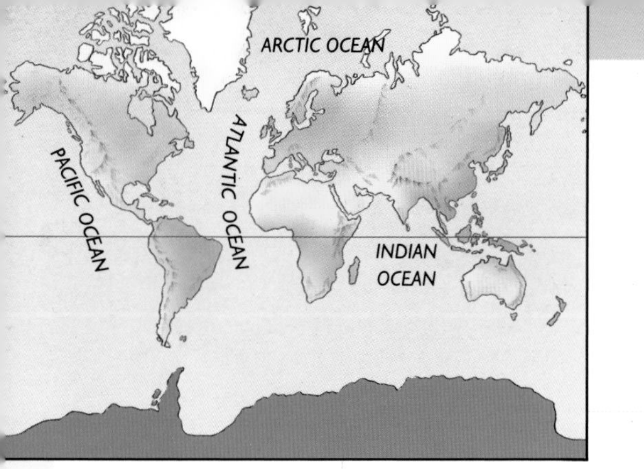


The extent of the Arctic and Antarctic ice varies from summer to winter. This ice is known as pack ice.

**Icebergs** are huge blocks of ice which float in the seas close to Antarctica and the Arctic. Most of an iceberg is hidden beneath the water. Icebergs can be very dangerous to ships.

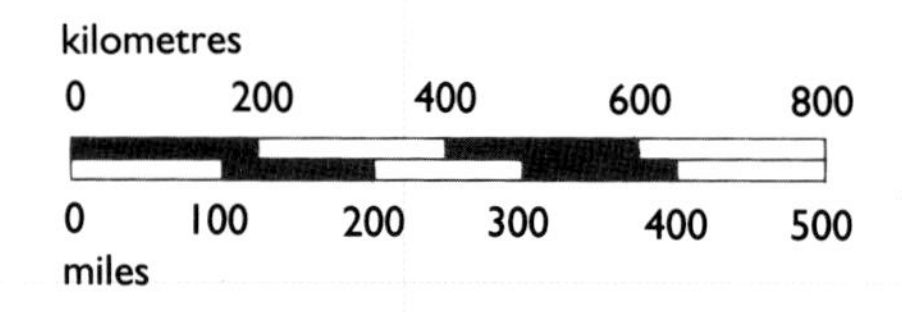


**The lowest temperature** ever recorded comes from the Vostok research station: 89° Centigrade below freezing. Antarctica is colder than the Arctic because the land takes longer to warm up in the summer sunlight.

**The Vinson Massif** is the highest mountain in Antarctica rising to 5,140 metres. Mount Erebus is the highest active volcano.

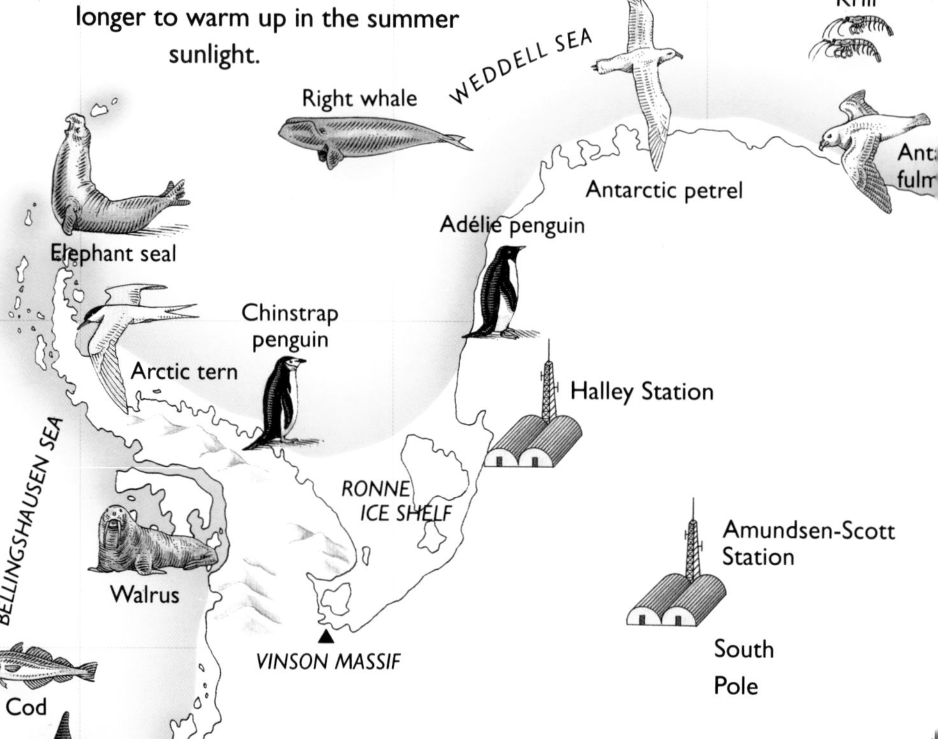

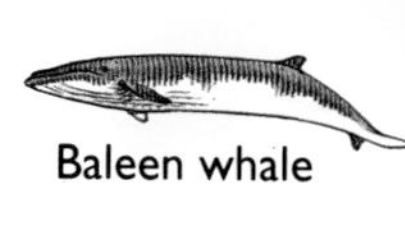

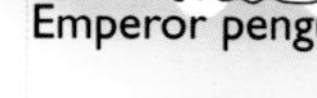


PACIFIC OCEAN

Baleen whale

## ANSWER THAT!

**1.** Which two kinds of seal are named after animals living in Africa?
**2.** Which stinging insect lives around the Arctic?
**3.** One kind of bird can be seen in both Antarctica and the Arctic because it flies from one to the other. What is its name?

**Penguins** are found only in the southern parts of the world, particularly around the edges of Antarctica. Emperor penguins are the largest kind. The males look after the eggs through the cold Antarctic winter and raise the young when they hatch.

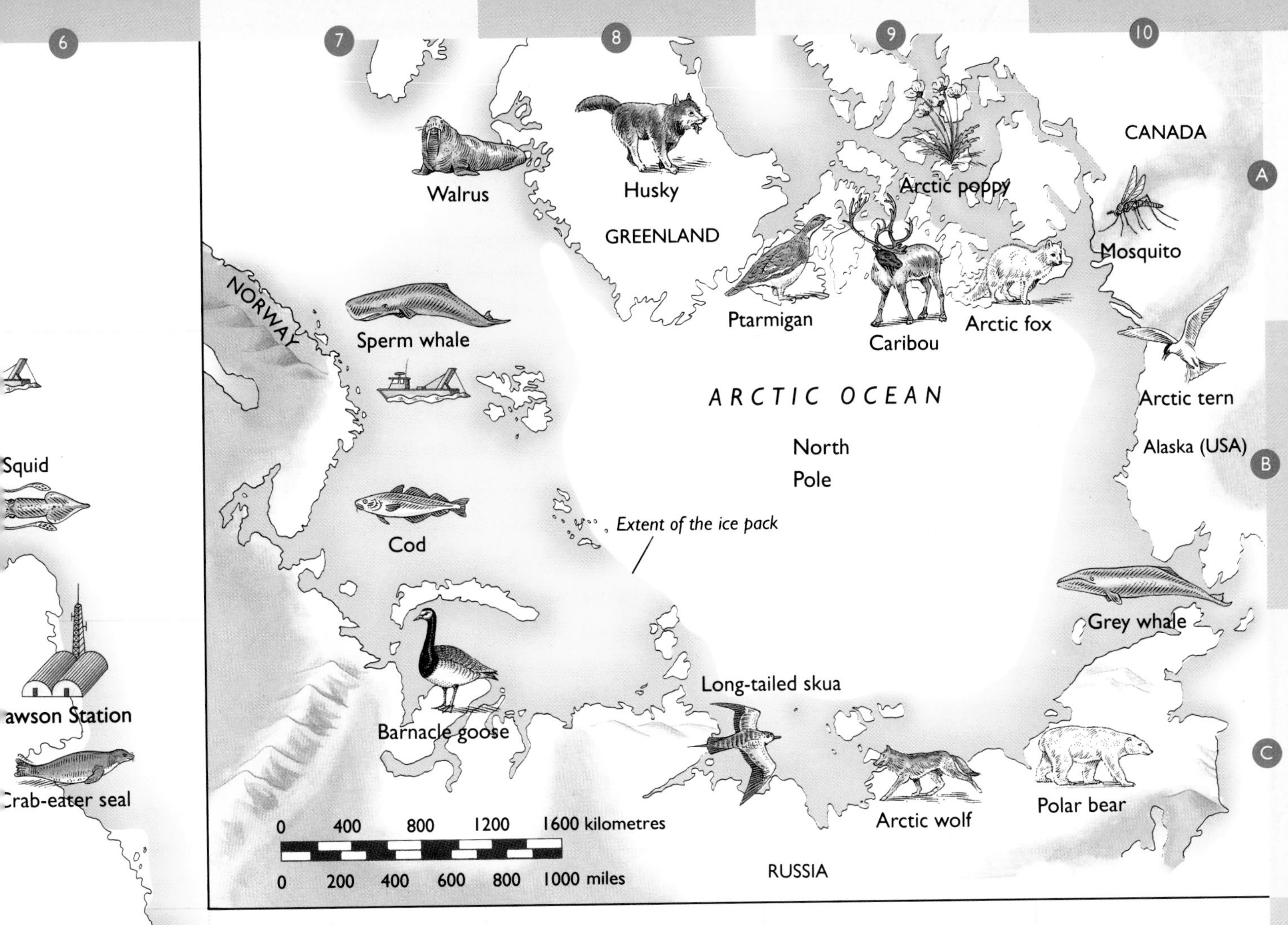


South Polar skua

INDIAN OCEAN

Casey Base

ard seal

**Scientific stations** carry out research in various parts of Antarctica, usually during the short summer. The scientists study such things as weather patterns and animal life.

# Antarctica and the Arctic

The very top and bottom of the world are the places which receive the least sunlight, and in winter they get no sunlight at all. These regions are bitterly cold, and covered with thick layers of ice and snow. The furthest point south on our world is called the South Pole, and the furthest point north is called the North Pole.

The South Pole is actually on land, in the middle of the continent called Antarctica. The North Pole is not on land at all, but on a huge sheet of ice in the middle of the Arctic Ocean. The size of the ice sheet changes as the ice melts and freezes during the year. The Inuit live around the edge of the Arctic. The only people in Antarctica are explorers and scientists.

# Flags of the World

## North America

CANADA

UNITED STATES OF AMERICA

MEXICO

GUATEMALA

BELIZE

EL SALVADOR

HONDURAS

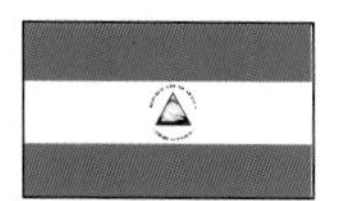

NICARAGUA

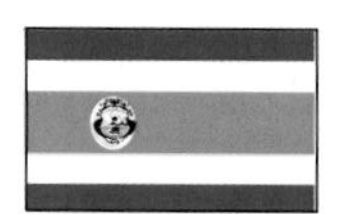

COSTA RICA

PANAMA

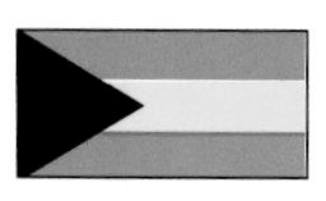

BAHAMAS

CUBA

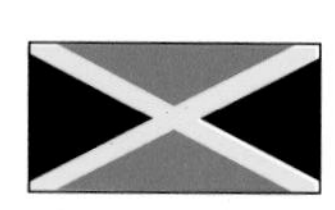

JAMAICA

HAITI

DOMINICAN REPUBLIC

ANTIGUA AND BARBUDA

ST KITTS AND NEVIS

DOMINICA

ST LUCIA

BARBADOS

GRENADA

ST VINCENT AND THE GRENADINES

TRINIDAD AND TOBAGO

## South America

VENEZUELA

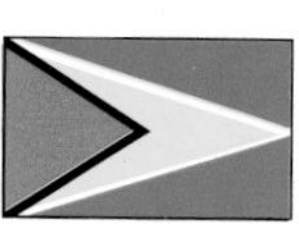

GUYANA

SURINAM

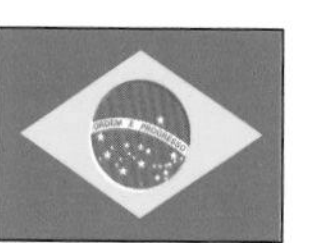

BRAZIL

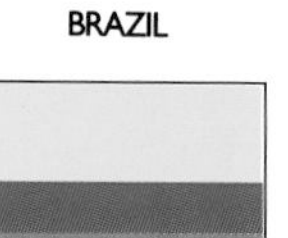

COLOMBIA

ECUADOR

PERU

BOLIVIA

PARAGUAY

URUGUAY

CHILE

ARGENTINA

## Europe

ICELAND

NORWAY

SWEDEN

FINLAND

DENMARK

IRELAND

UNITED KINGDOM

NETHERLANDS

BELGIUM

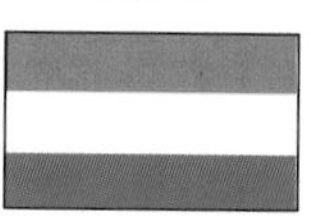

LUXEMBOURG

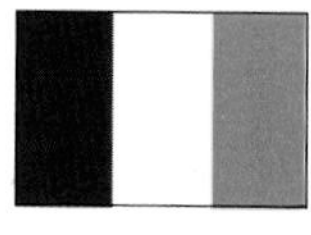

FRANCE

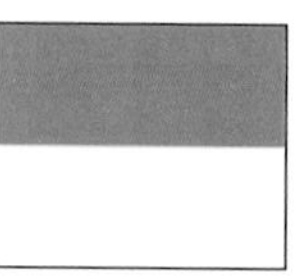

MONACO

SPAIN

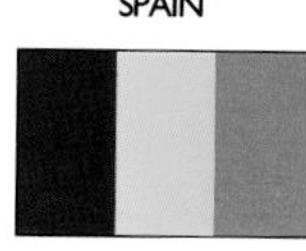
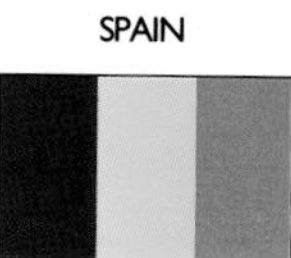

ANDORRA

PORTUGAL

ITALY

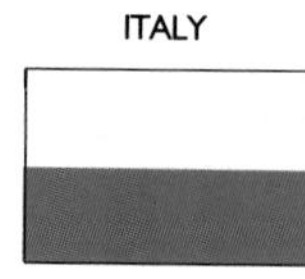
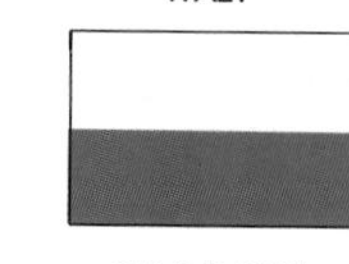

SAN MARINO

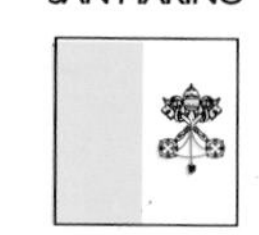

VATICAN CITY STATE

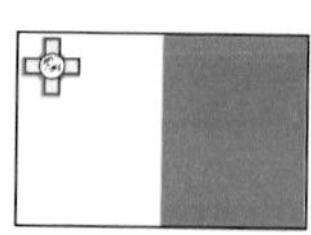

MALTA

SWITZERLAND

LIECHTENSTEIN

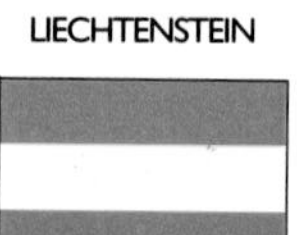

AUSTRIA

GERMANY

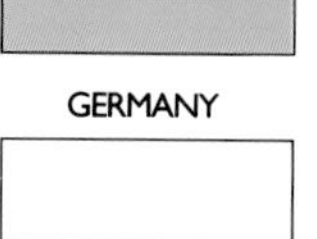

POLAND

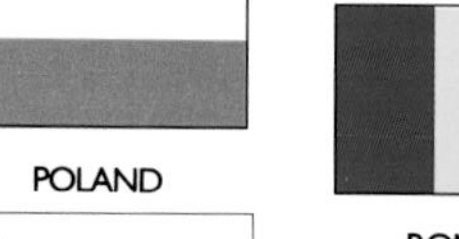

CZECH REPUBLIC

SLOVAKIA

HUNGARY

SLOVENIA

CROATIA

BOSNIA-HERZEGOVINA

YUGOSLAVIA

MACEDONIA

ALBANIA

GREECE

BULGARIA

ROMANIA

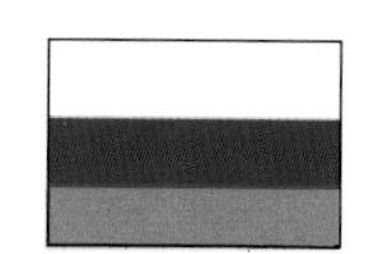

RUSSIA

ESTONIA

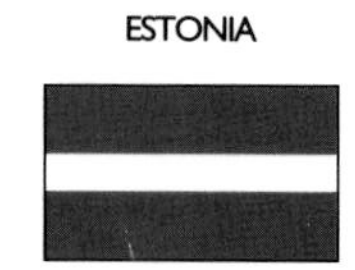

LATVIA

LITHUANIA

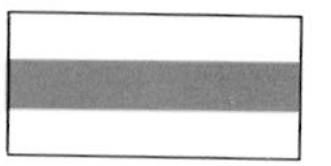

BELARUS

UKRAINE

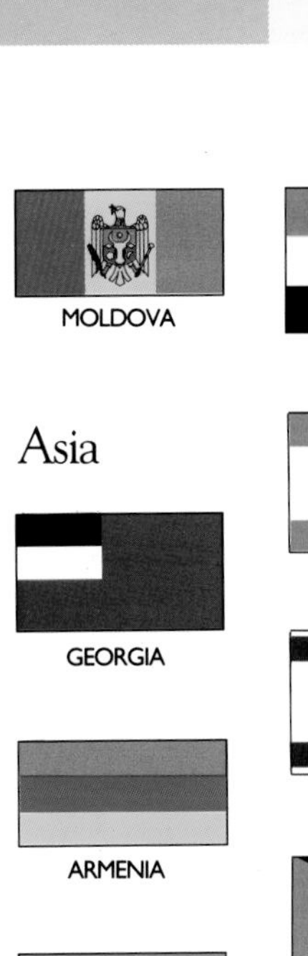

MOLDOVA

## Asia

GEORGIA

ARMENIA

AZERBAIJAN

KAZAKHSTAN

TURKMENISTAN

UZBEKISTAN

TAJIKISTAN

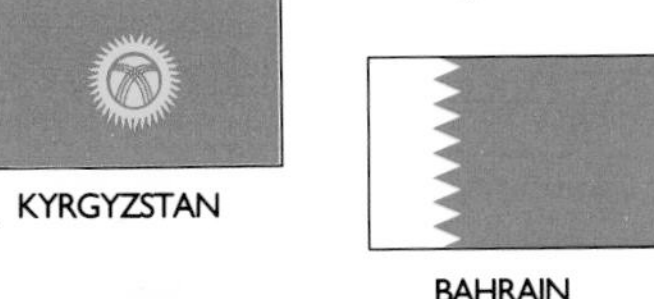

KYRGYZSTAN

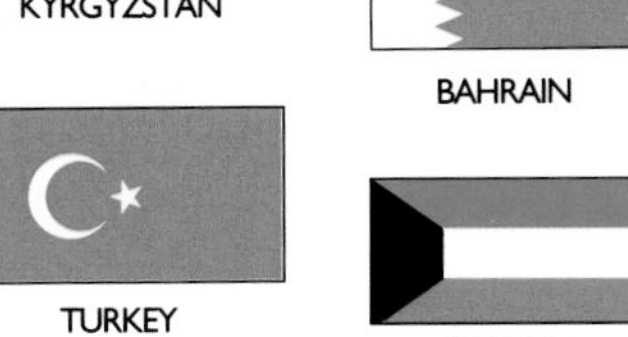

TURKEY

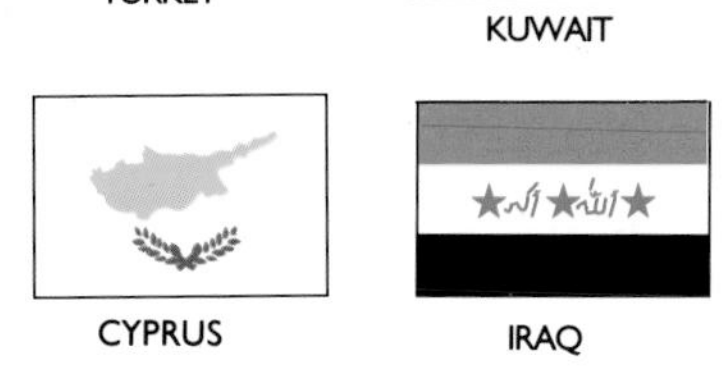

CYPRUS

SYRIA

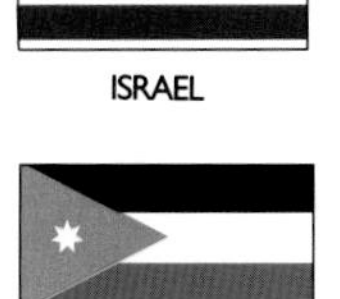

LEBANON

ISRAEL

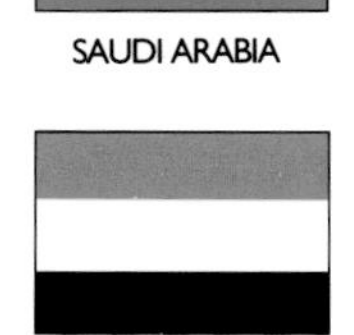

JORDAN

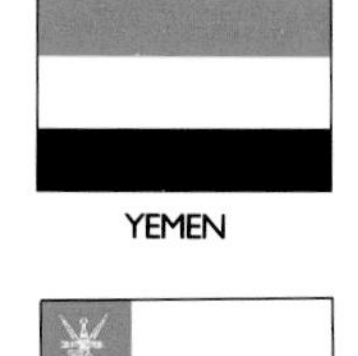

SAUDI ARABIA

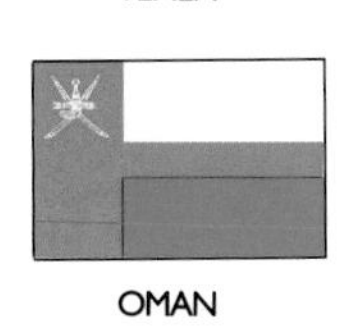

YEMEN

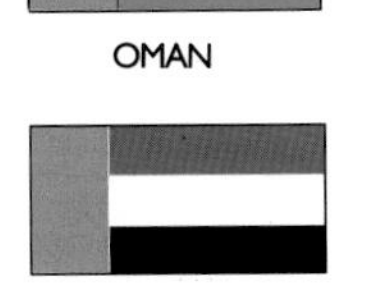

OMAN

UNITED ARAB EMIRATES

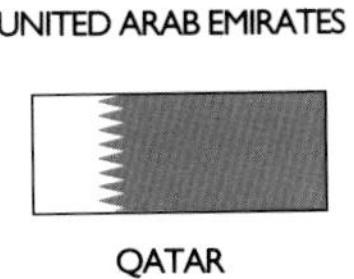

QATAR

BAHRAIN

KUWAIT

IRAQ

IRAN

AFGHANISTAN

PAKISTAN

INDIA

NEPAL

BHUTAN

BANGLADESH

SRI LANKA

MALDIVES

BURMA (MYANMAR)

THAILAND

CAMBODIA

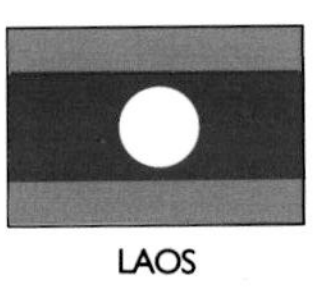

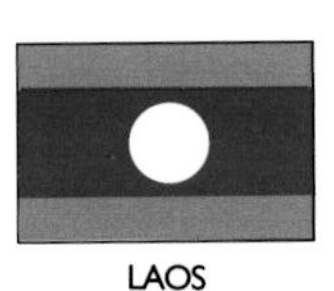

LAOS

VIETNAM

CHINA

MONGOLIA

NORTH KOREA

SOUTH KOREA

JAPAN

TAIWAN

PHILIPPINES

BRUNEI

MALAYSIA

SINGAPORE

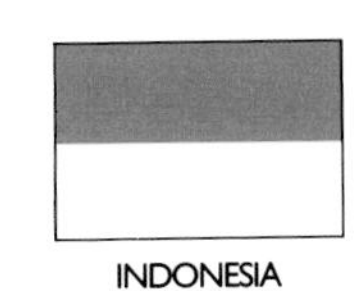

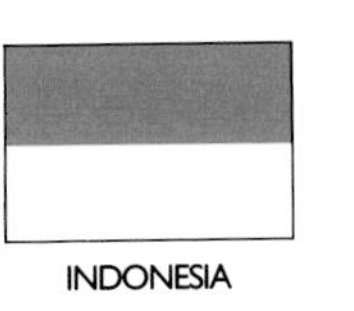

INDONESIA

## Africa

MOROCCO

ALGERIA

TUNISIA

MAURITANIA

SENEGAL

GAMBIA

GUINEA-BISSAU

GUINEA

SIERRA LEONE

LIBERIA

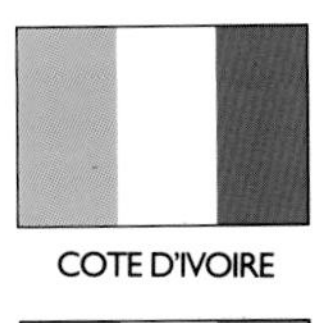

COTE D'IVOIRE

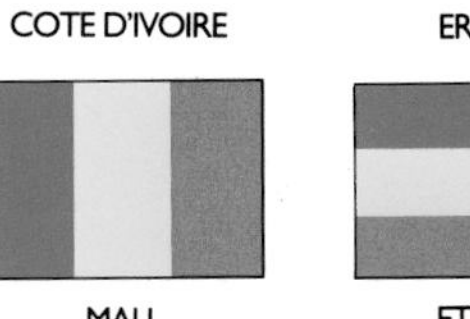

MALI

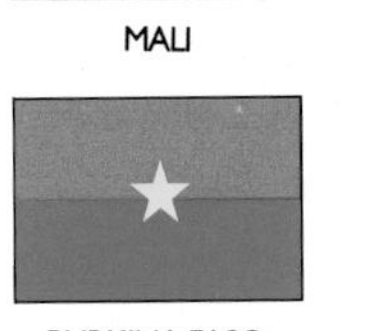

BURKINA FASO

GHANA

TOGO

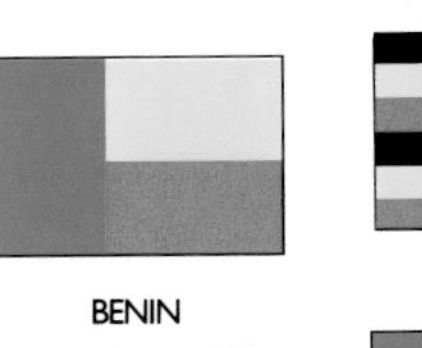

BENIN

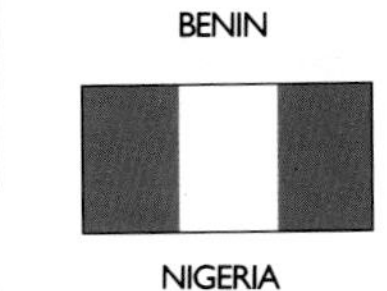

NIGERIA

NIGER

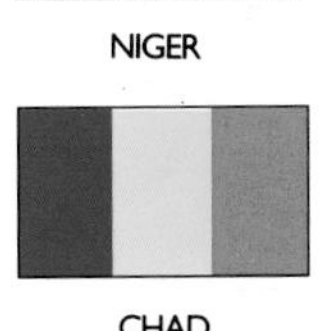

CHAD

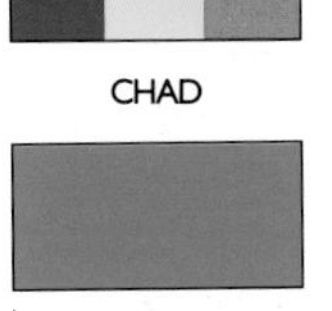

LIBYA

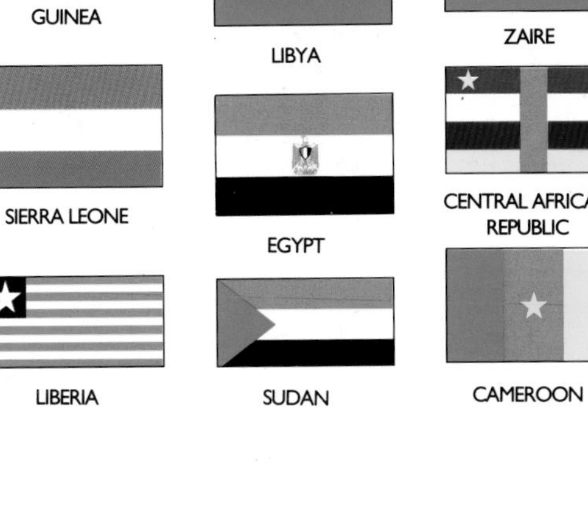

EGYPT

SUDAN

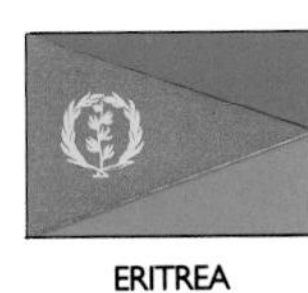

ERITREA

ETHIOPIA

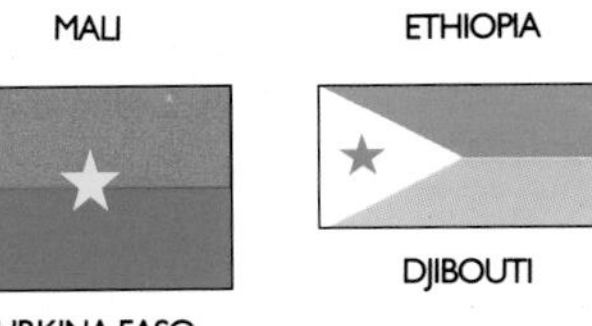

DJIBOUTI

SOMALIA

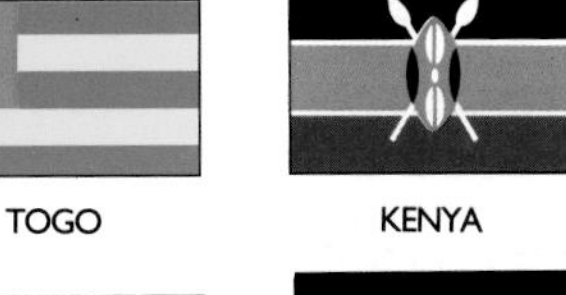

KENYA

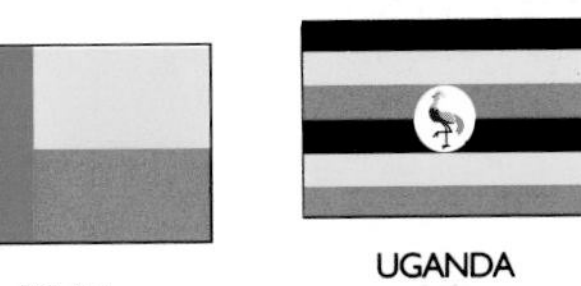

UGANDA

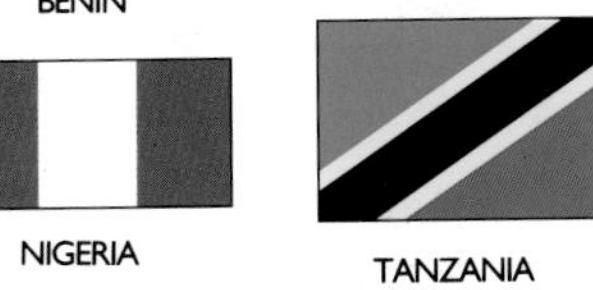

TANZANIA

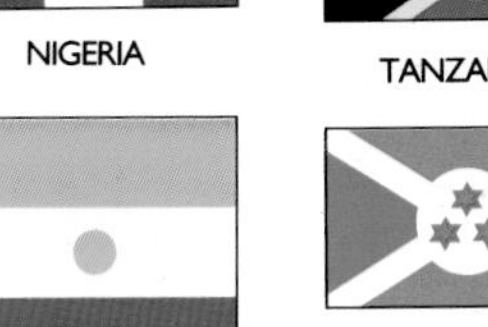

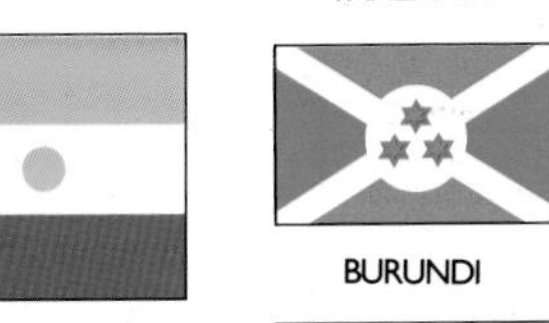

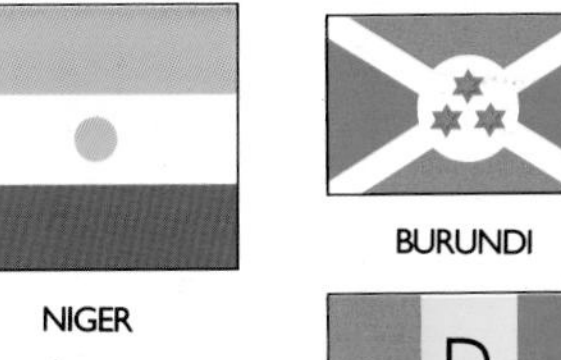

BURUNDI

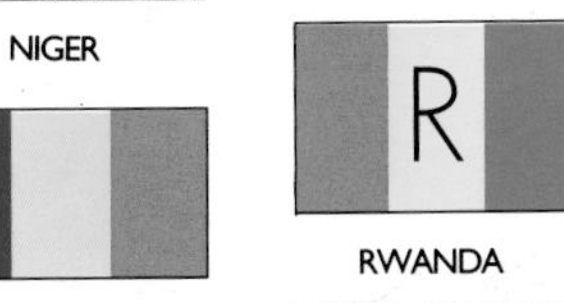

RWANDA

ZAIRE

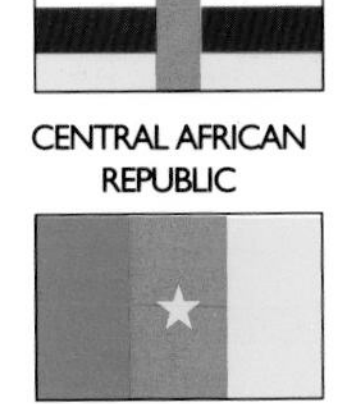

CENTRAL AFRICAN REPUBLIC

CAMEROON

EQUATORIAL GUINEA

GABON

SAO TOME AND PRINCIPE

CONGO

ANGOLA

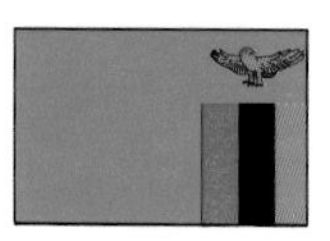
ZAMBIA

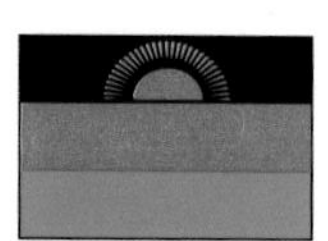
MALAWI

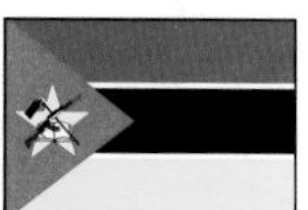
MOZAMBIQUE

ZIMBABWE

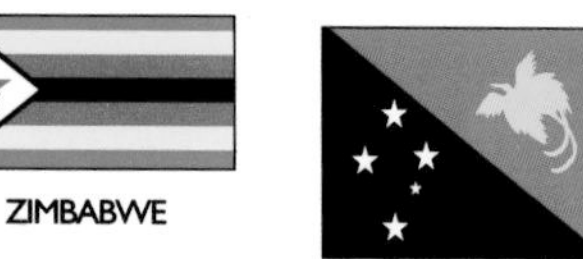

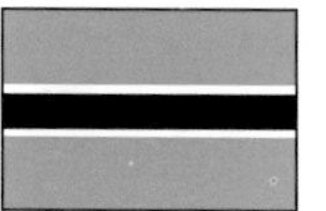
BOTSWANA

NAMIBIA

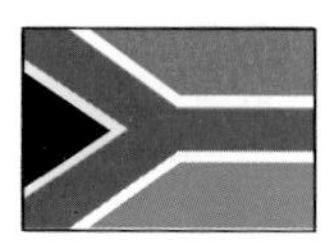
SOUTH AFRICA

LESOTHO

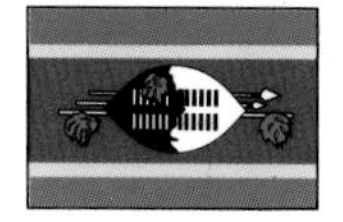
SWAZILAND

MADAGASCAR

CAPE VERDE

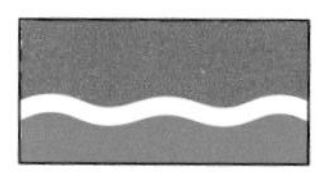
SEYCHELLES

COMOROS

MAURITIUS

## Australia and the Pacific

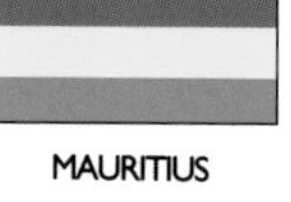
PAPUA NEW GUINEA

AUSTRALIA

NEW ZEALAND

FEDERATED STATES OF MICRONESIA

MARSHALL ISLANDS

SOLOMON ISLANDS

NAURU

TUVALU

KIRIBATI

VANUATU

FIJI

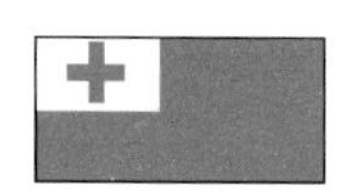
TONGA

WESTERN SAMOA

## ANSWER THAT!

*page 11*
**1.** Mexico
**2.** Cuba
**3.** Greenland

*page 13*
**1.** Narwhal
**2.** Maize (sweet corn)
**3.** Rattlesnake

*page 15*
**1.** Two, Brazil and Bolivia
**2.** Chile
**3.** Colombia

*page 16*
**1.** Sloth
**2.** Giant anteater
**3.** Poison arrow frog

*page 19*
**1.** Iceland
**2.** Istanbul in Turkey
**3.** Czech Republic

*page 21*
**1.** Pelican
**2.** Northern Russia
**3.** Chamois, in the Alps

*page 23*
**1.** Russia
**2.** New Delhi
**3.** Philippines

*page 24*
**1.** Bactrian camel
**2.** India
**3.** Java (Indonesia)

*page 27*
**1.** Abuja (it used to be Lagos)
**2.** Zaire, Zambia and Zimbabwe
**3.** Gambia

*page 28*
**1.** Chameleon
**2.** Camel
**3.** Aardvark

*page 30*
**1.** Canberra
**2.** Polynesia
**3.** North Island

*page 32*
**1.** Black
**2.** Ayers Rock
**3.** Kiwi (the national symbol of New Zealand) and Kakapo

*page 34*
**1.** Leopard seal and Elephant seal
**2.** Mosquito
**3.** Arctic tern

Now you have answered all these questions, here are some other kinds of questions to ask.

*What is the capital of...?*
*Which is the largest country in...?*
*Which is the smallest country in...?*
*Where is the highest mountain in...?*
*Where is the longest river in...?*

# Index

## A



## B



## C



## D



## E



## F



## G



## H



## I



## J



## K



## L